DUYGU TURGUT GÖKPINAR

MODERN PUNCH NEEDLE

22 MODERN PUNCH NEEDLE PROJECTS

2 PATTERN SHEETS • SAME-SIZE MOTIFS • VIDEO SUPPORTED TECHNIQUES

Tuva

Tuva Publishing
www.tuvapublishing.com

Adress Merkez Mah. Cavusbasi Cad. No:71
Cekmekoy - Istanbul 34782 / Turkey
Tel: 0216 642 62 62

Modern Punch Needle

First Print 2021 / October

All Global Copyrights Belong To

Tuva Tekstil ve Yayıncılık Ltd.

Content Embroidery

Editor in Chief Ayhan DEMİRPEHLİVAN
Project Editor Kader DEMİRPEHLİVAN
Designer Duygu Turgut GÖKPINAR
Project Assisstants Nur Efşan ÖZTÜRK, Mehmet KURT
Tehnical Editors Leyla ARAS, Büşra ESER
Text Editor Caroline SMITH
Graphic Designers Ömer ALP, Abdullah BAYRAKÇI,
Tarık TOKGÖZ

ISBN 978-605-7834-67-6

DO IT
FOR
YOUR
SELF

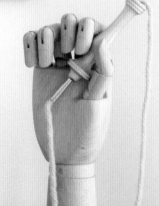

4

CONTENTS

MATERIALS   10

GETTING STARTED   20

PROJECTS

PROJECT GALLERY

Ethnic Patterned Cushion »**Page 32**

Geometric Wall Hanging »**Page 36**

Pot Holder »**Page 40**

Tote Bag »**Page 44**

Butterfly Rug »**Page 48**

Wall Organiser »**Page 52**

Terrazzo Hair Clip »**Page 56**

Book Cover »**Page 60**

Garland »**Page 64**

Floral Embossed Cushion »**Page 68**

Lampshade »**Page 72**

Make-up Bag »**Page 76**

Cute Stuffed Cat »Page 80

Kids Backpack »Page 84

Rainbow Cushion »Page 88

Hanging Wall Banner »Page 92

Baby Blanket »Page 96

Table Runner »Page 100

Curtain Tie Back »Page 104

Coasters »Page 112

Pouffe with Pompoms »Page 116

Mirror »Page 108

INTRODUCTION

It's not unusual to see throwbacks to past trends in the worlds of fashion and home decor but such throwbacks also occur in the field of craft. A craft that enjoyed great popularity in days gone by can sometimes be forgotten, only to enjoy a revival as it's taken up again. My discovery of punch needle embroidery, which dates back to the Middle Ages, was thanks to such a revival. Although the history of punch needle is obscure, it's thought it is possible to trace its origins to rug hooking techniques in medieval times or even as far back as the ancient Egyptians. This age-old skill has been growing in popularity in the last 10 years and is now taking its place in contemporary craft again.

I have tried my hand at many different crafts over the years and would definitely call myself a 'DIY-er'. When I see something new, I want to try it out, but very few of the crafts I've had a go at have become a passion – until I met the punch needle! Little did I imagine that the punch needle I bought in order to shoot a video for my YouTube channel would turn out to be one of the loves of my life! Printed on the packaging of that first punch needle were these words "It is easy to start, impossible to stop!" – a statement that turned out to be completely true for me.

What impressed me the most about punch needle is the fact that there is no limit to the projects you can make and that you have the opportunity to work with many different materials. The punch needle that I bought about 3 years ago has now become an important part of my life; every day, I work at the technique to improve my skills. I've shared my experiences with hundreds of people through workshops in Turkey and abroad. However, since the number of people that I can reach this way is limited, I decided to write a book. I want to share my experience with more of you and show just how many different things you can make with punch needle embroidery.

I should point out that I am completely self taught and this book is based on my personal experience. The techniques described here and the materials I've used are those that work best for me. As you develop your own interest in punch needle and experiment with fabrics and threads, you will find your own favoured methods and materials.

In this book you will find 22 different project to make with a punch needle. These include items to decorate your home, such as cushions and wall hangings, or accessories like hair clips, bags and book covers. I love to make punch needle projects for my daughter, Ipek, who has always been an inspiration, so you will find some special projects for children's items here too. I hope that my experience with punch needle and the projects in this book will be an inspiration for you!

MATERIALS

In my punch needle workshops I like to tell attendees that if they find the right materials, they are very likely to be successful. Indeed, there are two important factors for successful punch needle embroidery. The first is to find the right fabric, needle and thread to match; the second is, of course to practice. In this section, I will give you some information about the materials I've used over the years and share my opinions about which materials are ideal, especially for beginners.

PUNCH NEEDLE

There are many different punch needles on the market. In general, needles can be divided into two groups – adjustable and fixed needles. With adjustable needles, you can get different lengths of stitch by changing the length of your needle. This is not the case with fixed needles where your stitches will always be at the same length. Within both groups there are needles suitable for different thicknesses of yarn.

What are the ideal features in a punch needle?

» The metal part of the punch needle should have no rough edges. A punch needle needs to be easily pushed into the fabric so any roughnesses of the metal could tear the fabric while working and cause problems.

» The handle should have an ergonomic design. You sometimes end up using a punch needle for several hours and, in order to avoid a repetitive strain injury, it's very important that you can hold it comfortably.

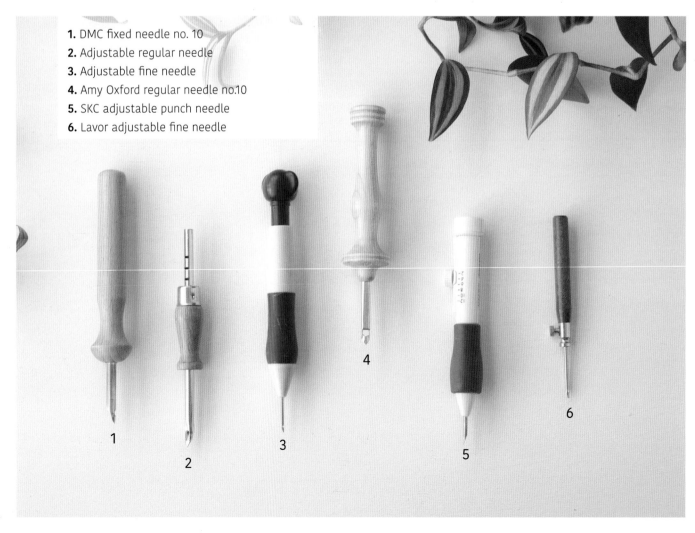

1. DMC fixed needle no. 10
2. Adjustable regular needle
3. Adjustable fine needle
4. Amy Oxford regular needle no.10
5. SKC adjustable punch needle
6. Lavor adjustable fine needle

THREAD/YARN

Depending on your punch needle, the thread or yarn use can vary. You can use a variety of different embroidery threads and you can use knitting or crochet yarn in weights from 2 ply (Fingering) through to Chunky (Bulky).

What should I consider when choosing a thread or yarn?

» The thread or yarn you choose for punch needle should move smoothly through your needle and should be fine enough to pass through the hole in the tip. If not, it will be difficult for you to get a neat finish as the yarn won't move through the needle comfortably.

» The make up of the thread or yarn you choose can depend on your intended project. For example, if I'm making something for children, I usually prefer cotton. If you're creating an item for someone with an allergy you might want to use an anti-allergic yarns. With these exceptions, there are no real restrictions about the type of thread or yarn as long as your choice is compatible with your needle. You can even turn a piece of fabric into your thread with a little bit of ingenuity.

FABRIC

It's important to match your fabric to your needle and thread or yarn if you want a great finished result. I've experimented with many different fabrics over the years and have found that the most suitable for punch needle is linen. The fabrics I use most are embroidery linen, raw linen, duck linen and monk's cloth.

You can also use aida or burlap, but as these have a more open weave that other fabrics and so have larger holes between the warp and weft threads, beginners may have difficulty working with them.

What are the main factors when choosing a fabric?

» The weave of your fabric should have gaps between the warp and weft threads that are big enough for the punch needle to pass through but small enough to hold onto the thread left by the punch needle. For fabrics with a finer weave, such as embroidery or duck linen, use a finer needle; for fabrics with a more open weave, like burlap, use a thicker needle.

» Because pressure is applied to a fabric as you use a punch needle it's best to avoid materials that are stretchy.

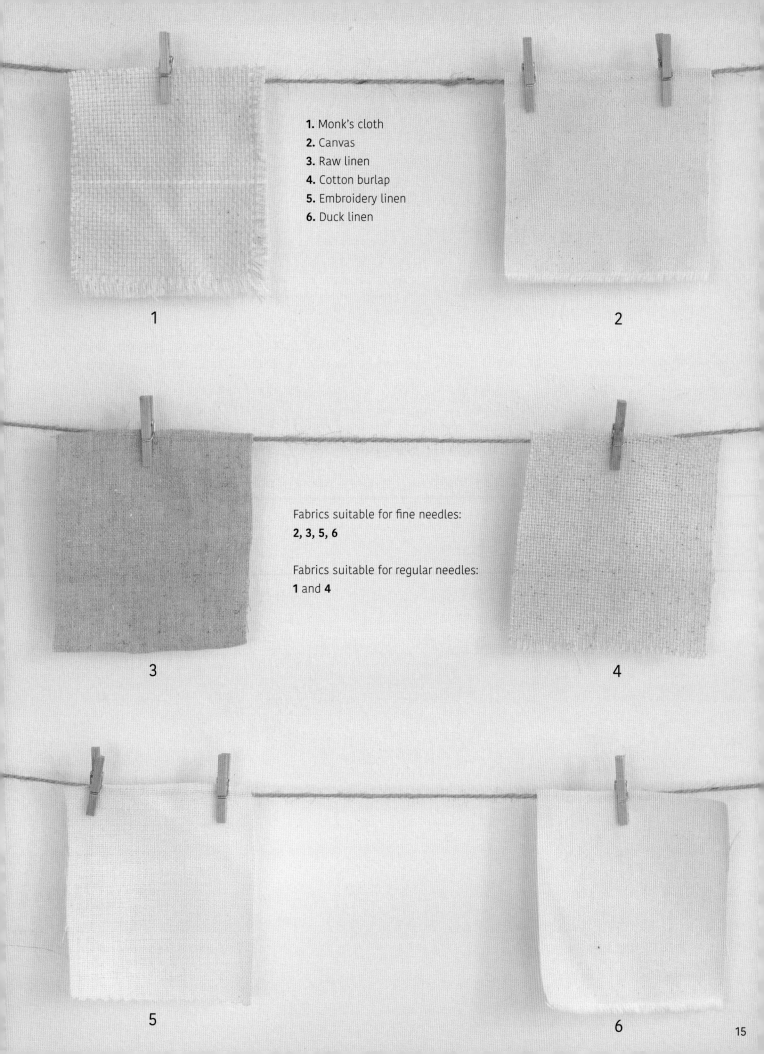

1. Monk's cloth
2. Canvas
3. Raw linen
4. Cotton burlap
5. Embroidery linen
6. Duck linen

Fabrics suitable for fine needles:
2, 3, 5, 6

Fabrics suitable for regular needles:
1 and **4**

1

2

3

4

5

6

FRAME

There are many different hoops and frames that you can use in punch needle embroidery. When I was a beginner I used round embroidery hoops as they were easily found in craft stores. These hoops may be preferred by some but there can be a few problems that should be taken into account. In my experience, round hoops were a little disappointing; as I punched the needle into the fabric I found it often came off the hoop and I could not get the exact tension I wanted. Moreover, working on a large scale project was time consuming with a small round hoop. That's why I turned to the wooden frames that are often used by those who are interested in punch needle embroidery, stretching my fabric onto the frame with the help of a staple gun. I can say that this has been one of my favoured methods since then.

What are the key features of a frame for punch needle embroidery?

» In punch needle embroidery, the more taut your fabric is, the easier it will be push the needle in. Using a staple gun can help you to get a fabric properly stretched on a frame. If you do not have a staple gun then you can hammer pins around the frame's edges to secure the fabric. I recommend using wooden frames, especially for larger projects. Although it might be difficult to find these wooden frames in stores, it is possible to make your own in the size you want. You can even use a photo frame or the frame of a painting canvas for this purpose.

» If you are going to work on smaller projects or embroider only a certain part of the fabric, you can use round embroidery hoops, which are widely available. There is a silicone part in some plastic hoops that helps prevent fabric from coming off, but if you cannot find a plastic hoop and have to use a wooden one, I advise you to wrap the inner part with a strip of cloth to help the fabric stretch better.

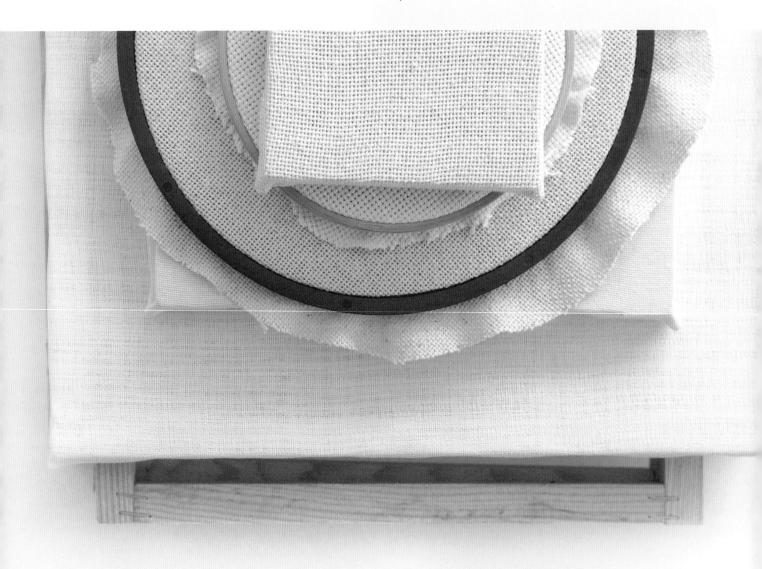

DESIGNS

When you are new to punch needle embroidery, you may have difficulty creating your own design. However, I think that there is another aspect that is as important as the design, and that is use of colour! Even the simplest geometric pattern can be transformed into a great project by the choice of harmonious colours. My advice, therefore, is to work on geometric patterns when you are a beginner. Simple shapes are easy to embroider and will be good practice. These types of patterns also give you a chance to play with colour combinations. As you continue to practice and your hand gets used to the punch needle, you will find it easier to fill in more detailed patterns and designs.

TOOLS

Finally, I would like to talk about the essential tools and equipment you need for punch needle embroidery. It's useful to have a pair of good-quality scissors while you work since you may need to cut the thread or yarn frequently as you change lengths or colours. If you are using a wooden frame you will need a staple gun to secure the fabric when you stretch it over the frame. When your embroidery is finished, you can use a staple remover to release your fabric from the frame. If you do not have one of these, you can use the tip of a screwdriver and a pair of pliers to gently ease out the staples. You should also have a threader to help thread your punch needle with yarn. This item is usually sold with a punch needle, but if yours is broken or lost, you you can make your own threader by folding a length of fine wire in half and attaching the ends to a button (see right).

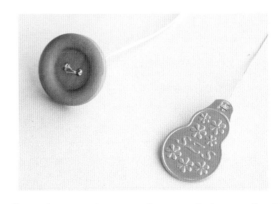

You will need a pencil to transfer your design to the fabric. A pencil or erasable fabric pen is the best choice. I don't recommend felt-tipped pens as they can leach onto the fabric easily. It may also be useful to have a ruler to help draw straight lines.

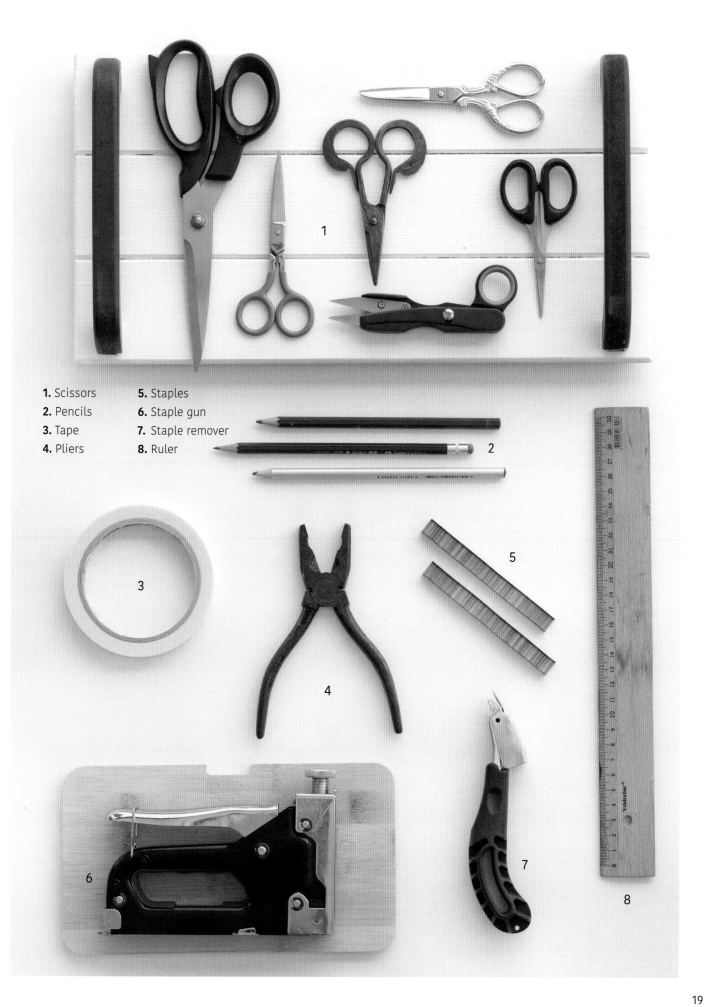

1. Scissors
2. Pencils
3. Tape
4. Pliers
5. Staples
6. Staple gun
7. Staple remover
8. Ruler

GETTING STARTED

In this section, I'm going to talk about what preparations you need to make before beginning your punch needle embroidery, and about what points you need to pay attention to while you work.

STRETCHING THE FABRIC ON THE FRAME

If you are going to use a wooden frame, you should cut your fabric so you have 5–10cm (2–4in) extra all round. This allows you to comfortably wrap the fabric around the frame and staple it in place. For example, if you are using a 40cm (16in) square frame, you should cut your fabric to 50cm (20in) square.

Place your fabric right-side down on a table or other flat surface and centre the frame on top. Wrap the excess fabric around the edges of the frame and staple in place, stretching the fabric as you do so. While stretching the fabric keep it as taut as possible but avoid pulling it too much on one side or there may not be enough fabric left to staple the other side. If you do not have a staple gun, you can use a small hammer and panel pins or tacks.

If you are using a round embroidery hoop, cut your fabric 5–10cm (2–4in) larger. Place the inner part of your hoop on the table and put the fabric on top, right side up and with the hoop centred under the fabric. Place the outer part of the hoop on the fabric so it is over the inner hoop. Press the two hoop parts together so that the fabric is gripped between them. Tighten the screw with pliers.

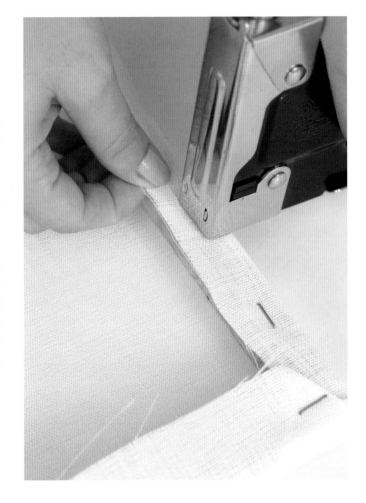

https://youtu.be/fvGxHA_23kg

After completing your embroidery, you can use a staple remover to take the staples out of the frame. If you do not have one, you can do this with a screwdriver and pliers. Gently lift the staples with the tip of the screwdriver, and then pull them out with pliers.

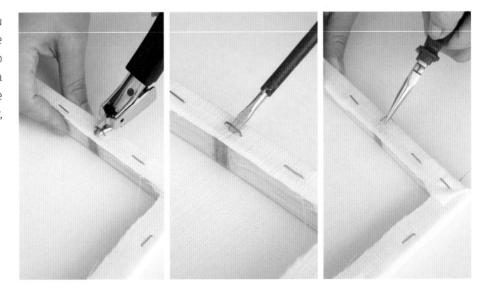

TRANSFERRING YOUR DESIGN TO THE FABRIC

Once you have stretched your fabric on a frame or hoop, the next step is to transfer your design to the fabric. Place the paper on which your design is drawn or printed under the fabric-covered frame. You can tape the edges of the paper to the fabric to secure it if liked. When you hold your frame up to a window or other light source, you will see that the lines on the paper will be visible through the fabric. You can then trace over the image with a pencil and so transfer your design to the fabric. I recommend a pencil for this because the ink from a felt-tip pen can easily spread outside the drawn line. If you are using a thicker fabric, it may be difficult to see the image clearly, even if you hold it up to a light source. In such cases, you can use carbon paper to transfer the template to the fabric. Place your frame on a flat surface, put the carbon paper on top and put your design on top of that, then go over the image with a pencil, pressing down to transfer the lines to your fabric.

MIRROR EFFECT

There are two sides to a piece of punch needle embroidery. On the side facing you as you work, the stitches will lie flat on the surface; on the underside of your work, the thread will form loops, giving a fluffy texture. If you want the fluffy side of the work to be the right side of the finished piece, you need to think carefully when transferring a design that features text or numbers: flip them so that they appear the wrong way round on the side on which you are working but the right way round on the fluffy side.

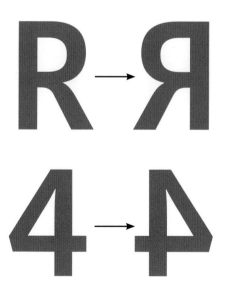

https://www.youtube.com/watch?v=NEqYmfoxzz4

THREADING THE PUNCH NEEDLE

Some punch needles are threaded by using a wire threader, while others simply have a slot along the needle through which we thread the yarn. In my workshops, I've noticed that some beginners can find threading the punch needle a little complicated at first, but with practice it soon gets easier.

https://youtu.be/-ZtbTkGEQhE

USING A THREADER

1. Insert the tip of the threader into the tip of the hollow punch needle and let it move completely through the needle until it comes out at the back of the handle.

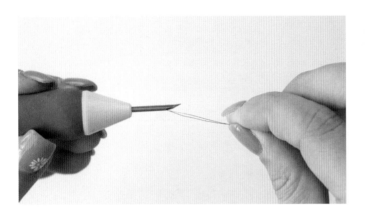
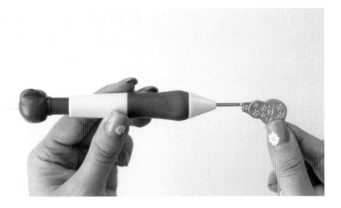

2. Open up the loop of wire at the tip of the threader and slip your yarn through it. Pull the other end of the threader so the yarn is drawn back through the handle and along the hollow punch needle to emerge at its tip.

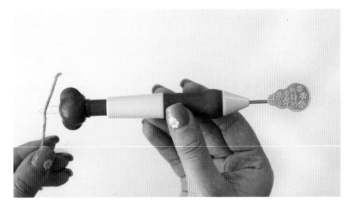

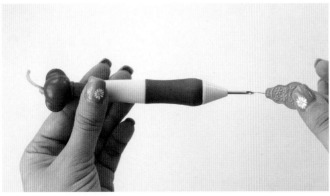
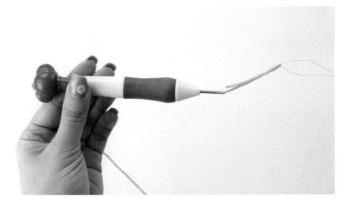

3. Remove the yarn from the threader, then insert the tip of the threader in the eye in the tip of the punch needle. Slip your yarn through the threader again and then use the threader to draw the yarn through the eye of the needle.

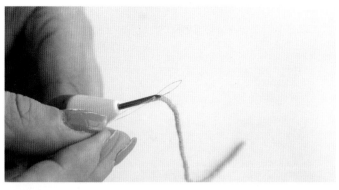
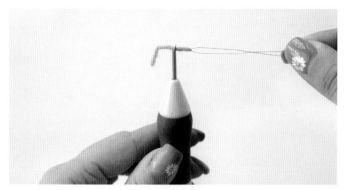

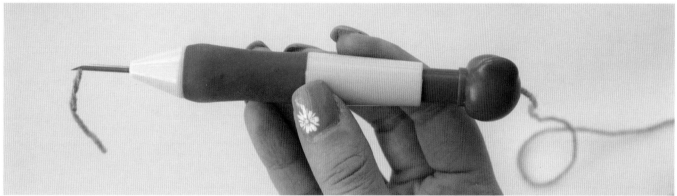

If you lose or break your threader you can make one by folding a length of fine wire in half and then attaching the ends to a button. Make sure that the folded length of wire is longer than the length of your punch needle.

THREADING WITHOUT A THREADER

Some punch needles, like the Oxford, have a slot all the way along the handle and needle shaft. You simply draw your yarn along the slot and then thread it through the needle eye.

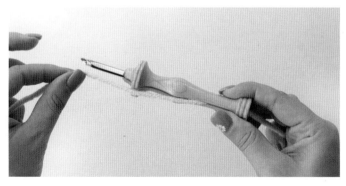

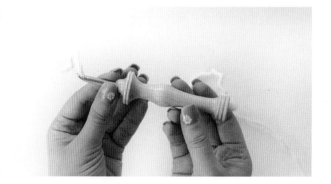

STARTING

Hold your needle as if you are holding a pencil. Place the tip of the needle on the fabric with the yarn lying across the surface. Push the needle into the fabric so the full length of the metal shaft goes all the way through and the handle touches the surface of the fabric.

https://youtu.be/O_6W-Yd7x6A

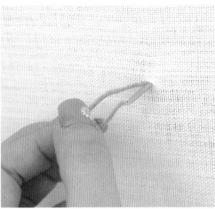
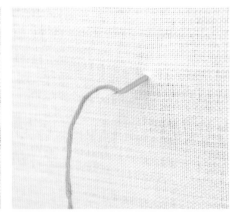

Turn your work over so you can see the needle on the other side. Use your fingers to pull the end of the yarn through so a length hangs down at the back. This is your 'starter thread' and pulling it through in this way reduces the risk of it working loose.

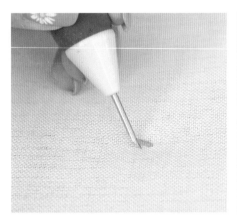

Draw your needle out of the fabric but not too far – keep the tip just touching the surface. Move the tip of the needle on to the position for the next stitch and push it through the fabric again. As you do so, do not lift the needle up high – allow it to brush over the surface of the fabric as you work.

Every time you punch the needle into the fabric, you create a stitch. The ideal density of stitches is to work four for every 1cm (⅜in) with a fine needle, and two stitches for every 1cm (⅜in) with a regular needle. If your stitches are too close together, you will end up with a tangled look in the fluffy part on the other side of the fabric. If your stitches are too far apart, there will be gaps between the loops in the fluffy side.

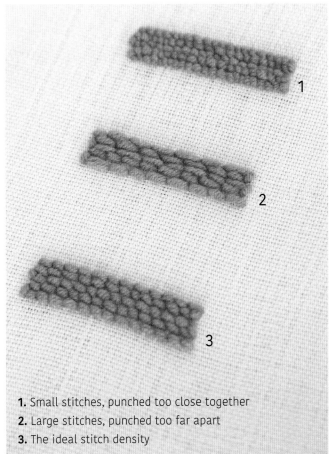

1. Small stitches, punched too close together
2. Large stitches, punched too far apart
3. The ideal stitch density

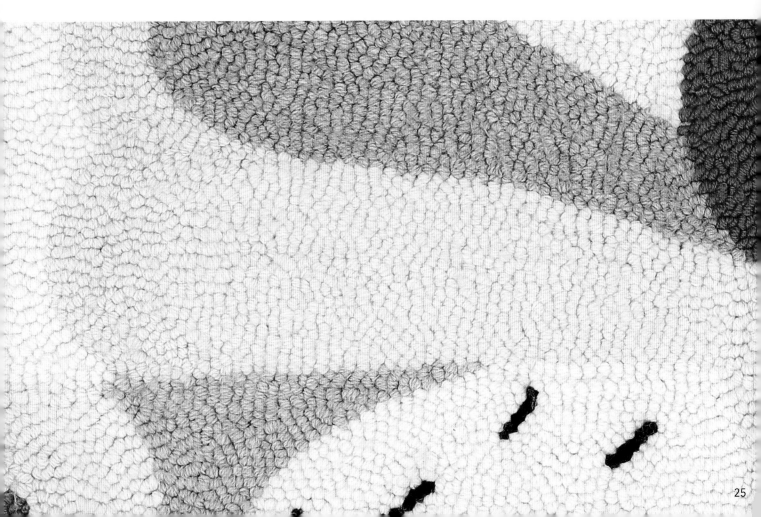

NEEDLE ADJUSTMENT

Adjustable needles allow you to change the length of the metal needle shaft so you can make the loops on the fluffy side of your work the desired length. There are a few important points to bear in mind here. The first one is about the amount of yarn used; the higher the setting of your needle, the larger the loops you will get at the back, which means more thread is used. If the flat side of embroidery is to be your right side, you can set the needle so that the loops are shorter and so avoid unnecessary thread use. The second point worth mentioning regards the look on the fluffy side. When your needle is set to a high length, you will get longer loops that tend mingle with each other and look more messy. With a lower length, the loops will form a neater pile. If loops get tangled up, you can separate them with the tip of your needle when the embroidery is complete.

Since you cannot make adjustments to a fixed needle, the loops on the fluffy side of your embroidery will always be the same length.

FILLING IN A SHAPE

There are many ways in which you can fill in a shape in punch needle embroidery, and the method you use may depend on your project. My main advice is to follow the outline of the shape as you work. For example, if you are filling in a triangle, start by embroidering around its outline, then fill it in with smaller triangles, working inwards.

When filling in an irregular shape, such as a cloud, you should follow the same method, embroidering the outline first, then filling in it by following this outline, working inwards. If you work in rows your finished shape may not have smooth edges.

There are also other techniques that you can use to add dynamism to your embroidery such as working from right to left or up and down, or by cutting the ends of the fluffy loops.

If your design consists of shapes within shapes, you should first fill the inner elements and then embroider the outer ones. For example, in a teddy bear, you should first embroider elements such as the eyes, nose and cheeks, then move on to filling the rest of the face. I like to call this the inside-out rule.

https://youtu.be/QC1Q1F76AQE

BRICK METHOD

In this technique, it's the flat side of the embroidery rather than the fluffy one that is the right side. After working a first row of evenly spaced, straight stitches, move on to the next row and this time, punch the needle into the fabric at the middle of the stitches of the previous row.

https://youtu.be/k4yh0tiHjtY

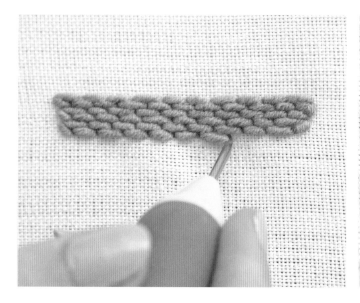

RUG METHOD (or CUT PILE METHOD)

If you have an adjustable needle, set it so you will make longer loops on the fluffy side. With a fixed needle, you will need to get hold of the yarn at the back of the fabric every time you insert the needle and pull a bit of yarn through. When you've finished the work, you can cut the ends of all the loops; after you've brushed the work with your hand it will have the look of a rug pile.

https://youtu.be/0RS-EEp4yGk

TRIMMING THE YARN

When you have finished working or you want to change yarn, punch the needle to finish the last stitch but do not lift it out. Use your hand to get hold of the yarn at the back of your work – just hold it, do not pull it – then lift the needle out at the front, away from the fabric, and cut the yarn.

https://youtu.be/HUkjFMde_Jk

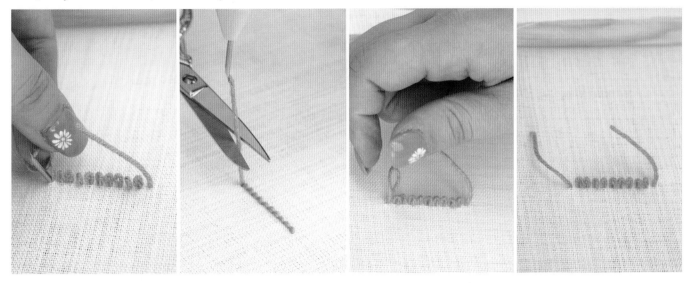

Once the thread is cut, pull the loop that you were holding onto at the back through to that side. Both the starting and finishing ends of yarn will be on the fluffy side.

When you've finished your embroidery, trim any starting or finishing threads to the same length as the fluffy loops.

Depending on your project, either the flat or fluffy side of your work can be the right side of your finished piece, but you can also combine both flat and fluffy on the same surface for a more dynamic look.

ETHNIC PATTERNED CUSHION

The combination of modern and ethnic patterns has always excited me. I find that when ethnic patterns are used in accessories such as carpets, rugs and cushions, they soften the modern style and create a warmer look. For this project, I've used ethnic-inspired geometric patterns that I think will add a positive energy to your home. I've created a longer, more pillow-like shape, rather than a classic square cushion, and you can use it both on your bed and in the living room. I also used the rug method (see page 28) on some parts of the design to give you a chance to try this technique and to add a little more interest to the finished piece.

MATERIALS & TOOLS

» Monk's cloth, 45 x 75cm (18 x 30in)
» Wooden frame, 35 x 65cm (14 x 25in)
» Oxford punch needle, no. 10
» Yarn – Chunky/Bulky weight, *see Chart for suggestions, colours and amounts*
» Scissors
» Staple gun
» Staple remover or screwdriver and pliers
» Pen
» Design template - sheet 1A
» Fabric glue (optional)
» Zip, 30cm (12in)
» Linen or canvas fabric for the backing, 40 x 70cm (16 x 28in
» Sewing machine
» Iron
» Pins

YARN CHART			
COLOUR	BRAND/COMPANY	CODE	AMOUNT NEEDED
Beige	Kartopu Punto (Bulky/100g - 110m)	M000373	150g (5.3oz)
Pink	Kartopu Punto (Bulky/100g - 110m)	M374	30g (1oz)
Brown	Kartopu Cozy Wool (Bulky/100g - 110m)	K885	30g (1oz)
Dusty Rose	Himalaya Snow (Bulky/100g - 107m)	755-11	50g (1.75oz)

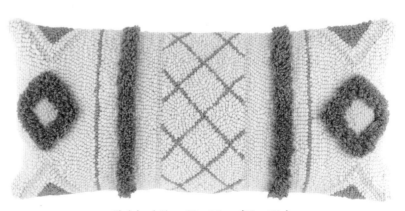

Finished Size: 60 x 30cm (24 x 12in)

EMBROIDERY

1 Using a staple gun, stretch the monk's cloth over the wooden frame. The frame for this project is quite large, so make sure the fabric is evenly stretched (see page 20). Monk's cloth can fray easily at the edges, so cut your fabric 1–2cm (⅜–¾in) wider all round. A frame with the inside dimensions of 35 x 65cm (14 x 25in) will give you enough space to work comfortably.

2 Transfer your design to the fabric (see page 21). Monk's fabric is a little thicker than other embroidery linens, so if you have difficulty seeing the pattern clearly through the fabric when you place the design template under the frame and hold it up to the light, you can transfer the design using carbon paper. As you work with the punch needle, the lines made by the carbon paper can get broken up, so take care to make them strong and neat.

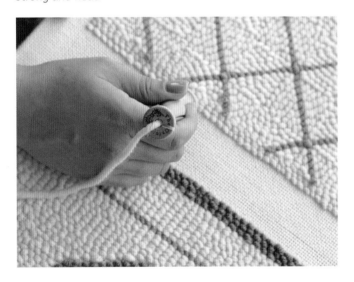

3 You can start from any point you wish, but if there are motifs within your design, start by filling in the inner shapes first. With this project, my advice is to start with the lattice pattern in the middle. For this area, thread your punch needle with brown yarn and embroider along the lines. If you are embroidering a single line you can make your stitches a little closer than usual so that there is no gap between the loops and you cannot see the fabric in between.

4 After completing the lines in the middle section, thread your punch needle with beige yarn and fill in the areas between the lines of the lattice pattern. When you've filled in each shape, cut your yarn and start afresh on the next shape. In punch needle embroidery, it's best not skip to another shape without cutting the yarn as it increases the risk of your embroidery stitches coming out.

5 When you've completed the middle section, thread your punch needle with pink yarn. Embroider two lines on either side of the middle section.

6 After embroidering the pink lines, thread the needle with beige again and embroider 10 lines on either side of the pink lines. You can do this in an 'up and down' way; that is, by punching your needle one line up and one line down. While doing this, make sure that the last loops in the upper and lower sections are in line.

7 Next, thread your punch needle with dusty rose coloured yarn. Insert your needle in the fabric, holding onto the yarn at the back with one hand as you gently pull your needle out of the fabric. Continue in the same way, holding the yarn with your hand each time you make a stitch in order to get longer loops in this section and so make the trimming process easier (see image A, page 35). Work three lines of dusty rose on each side.

8 Thread the punch needle with beige again and work ten lines up and down on either side. Then, using brown, work a single line on either side.

9 Using pink, outline the inside part of the diamond shapes, then fill them in. With dusty rose, outline the outer edge of the diamond shapes, holding the yarn at the back as in step 7 to get longer loops, then fill in this section in the same way. Using brown, outline the triangles, then fill in them. Use two lines of pink to outline the outer triangle shape, then fill in between with beige.

10 After filling in all the design, trim any strands that are left at the start and finish of a length of yarn so they are equal to the size of adjacent loops. Cut the ends of the longer loops that you made with the dusty rose coloured yarn (see A below), then trim to an even length (see B). Gently smooth this area with the palm of your hand.

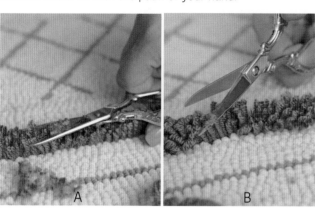

A   B

11 When your embroidery is finished, you can apply some fabric glue to the wrong side, then leave it to dry for 24 hours.

12 Remove your finished work from the frame using a staple remover or a screwdriver and pliers. Trim the edges of fabric, leaving a seam allowance of at least 3cm (1¼in) all round.

MAKING UP THE CUSHION

1 Lay your finished work out flat, right side up. Trim the canvas fabric for the backing so that it is 3cm (1¼in) larger all round than the embroidered piece.

2 Fold your backing fabric in half and cut along the fold. On one piece, turn under one short edge by 1cm and press it. Open the zip and place one side of it along the pressed edge; pin in place. Using a sewing machine, stitch in place.

3 Take the other piece of backing fabric and turn under and press one short edge. Pin the other side of the zip to the pressed edge then sew in place. Close the zip.

4 Bring the finished embroidery and the backing fabric right sides together. Open the zip by about 10cm (4in), then pin the two pieces together. Sew around the edges, keeping your stitching close to the embroidered stitches. It will help to use the zipper foot of your sewing machine, if it has one.

5 When you have finished sewing, trim off any excess fabric around the edges and snip across the corners to reduce bulk. If liked, you can stabilise the seam by adding zigzag stitching all round or by brushing on some fabric glue. Open the zip completely and turn the cushion cover to the right side through the gap. Push your finger into the corners to shape the cover into a rectangle.

GEOMETRIC WALL HANGING

Wall hangings are among the easiest projects you can create with a punch needle. With a modern design and contemporary colours, this simple hanging make can add a completely different vibe to your home. For this project, I have combined a range of different shapes that are easy to embroider. You can also finish your wall hanging with tassels or pompoms. Depending on the rest of your home decor, you could position this hanging both horizontally or vertically.

Finished Size: 22 x 42cm (8¾ x 16½in)

MATERIALS & TOOLS

» Monk's cloth, 35 x 45cm (14 x 18in)
» Wooden frame, 25 x 35cm (10 x 14in)
» Oxford punch needle, no. 10
» Yarn – Chunky/Bulky weight, *see Chart right for suggestions, colours and amounts*
» Scissors
» Staple gun
» Staple remover or screwdriver and pliers
» Pen
» Design template – sheet 1A
» Fabric glue (optional)
» Hot glue gun and silicone
» Wooden doweling rod – 1cm (⅜in) wide and 28cm (11in) long
» Cotton cord, for hanging
» Cardboard, 11cm square (4¼in square)

YARN CHART			
COLOUR	BRAND/COMPANY	CODE	AMOUNT NEEDED
Pink	Kartopu Cozy Wool (Bulky/100g - 110m)	K1873	15g (0.5oz)
Purple	Kartopu Cozy Wool (Bulky/100g - 110m)	K1707	15g (0.5oz)
Blue	Kartopu Cozy Wool (Bulky/100g - 110m)	K1533	10g (0.3oz)
Green	Kartopu Punto (Bulky/100g - 110m)	M448	10g (0.3oz)
Cream	Kartopu Punto (Bulky/100g - 110m)	M025	50g (1.75oz)
Black	Kartopu Punto (Bulky/100g - 110m)	K940	5g (0.17oz)
Light Blue	Kartopu Punto (Bulky/100g - 110m)	M385	10g (0.3oz)
Yellow	Alize Maxi (Super Bulky/100g - 100m)	2	15g (0.5oz)
Orange	Myboshi (Super Bulky/50g - 42m)	173	15g (0.5oz)

EMBROIDERY

1 Stretch your fabric over the wooden frame and secure using a staple gun (see page 20). Cut the monk's cloth 1–2cm (⅜–¾in) wider all round because it can fray easily. A frame with the inside dimensions of 25 x 35cm (10 x 14in) will be big enough for you to work comfortably.

2 Place your design template under the frame, taping it down around the edges if liked. Hold up the frame to a light source so you can see the design through the fabric and trace over it with a pencil (see page 21).

3 Thread your punch needle with the colour with which you would like to start. Where there are shapes within shapes, start by filling the inner ones first. For example, before embroidering the pink area, fill in the blue rectangle inside it. If you fill in the pink area first, the loops may cover the area to be filled with blue.

4 While embroidering a shape, first outline it then continue to fill it in by following that outline. For example, if you are going to embroider a triangle, I recommend you work the outline of the triangle first, then continue to fill in it by embroidering smaller triangles within that rather working back and forth in rows.

5 When filling in a shape, try to punch the needle closely together on each line so that the fabric between cannot be seen. After filling in all the shapes in this design you can embroider the background with cream yarn. I chose this colour to help the geometric shapes stand out.

6 Remove your finished work from the frame using a staple remover or a screwdriver and pliers. Trim the edges of fabric, leaving an allowance of at least 3cm (⅜in) at the edges and bottom and of at least 6cm (2¼in) at the top. If liked, brush fabric glue on the wrong side and leave to dry for 24 hours.

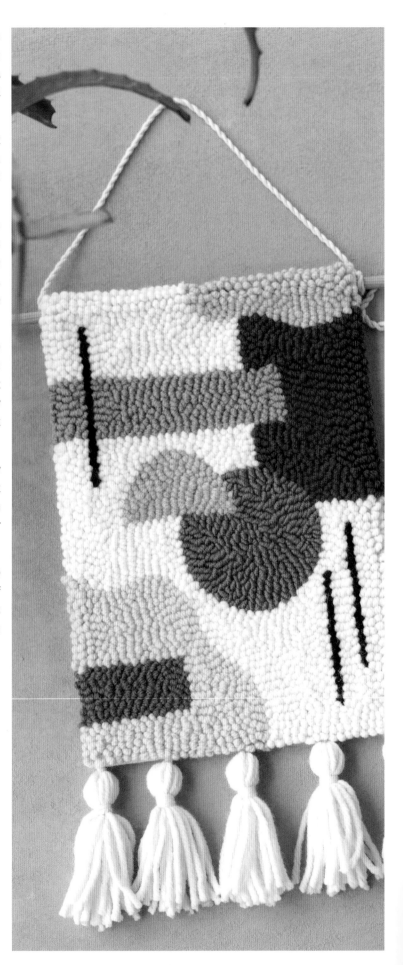

MAKING UP THE WALL HANGING

1 After removing your project from the frame, lay it out flat with the right side facing downwards. Meanwhile, set your hot glue gun to warm up. Fold under the edges of the work along the sides and bottom and glue in place with the hot glue gun. Place the doweling rod along the top edge and fold the fabric over it; use the hot glue gun to glue it in place.

2 To make the tassels, start by cutting out an 11cm (4¼in) square of cardboard. Wrap cream yarn about 15 times around the cardboard. Tie the beginning of the yarn to the end, then cut it off. Slip the loops off the cardboard. Cut a 15–20cm (6–8in) length of yarn and wrap it around the loops, about 2cm from one end; tie in a knot to draw the yarn into the tassel shape. Cut through the bottom of the loops then trim the strands to an equal length.

3 Make another four tassels then use matching yarn to sew them securely to the bottom edge of the wall hanging.

4 Cut a 55cm (21½in) length of cotton cord. Knot each end of the rope to each end of the dowelling to form the hanging loop for your finished piece.

POT HOLDER

Items that are embroidered with a punch needle are usually quite thick, thanks to the fluffy side, so this gave me an idea – I could use punch needle embroidery to make a pot holder without the need of any wadding. I designed these two pot holders in the shape of houses and completed each one with a leather strap. The straps form hanging loops for the pot holders but they also look like the chimneys. I'm sure they'll brighten up any kitchen. You could also use them as trivets, by making a slight change in the design and finishing them without straps.

Finished Size: House 1: 16 x 19cm (6¼ x 7½in)

Finished Size: House 2: 15 x 22cm (6 x 8¾in)

MATERIALS & TOOLS

» Two pieces of embroidery linen, each 25cm (10in) square
» Wooden frame, 20cm (8in) square
» Adjustable punch needle
» Yarn – DK/Light Worsted and 4 ply/Sport weight, *see Chart right for suggestions, colours and amounts*
» Scissors
» Staple gun
» Staple remover or screwdriver and pliers
» Pencil
» Design template – pages 121–122
» Sewing needle and thread
» Fabric glue (optional)
» Two leather straps, each 2.5cm (1in) wide and 24cm (9½in) long
» Two pieces of linen fabric or felt for the backing, 20cm (8in) square
» Hot glue gun and silicone

YARN CHART - HOUSE 1			
COLOUR	BRAND/COMPANY	CODE	AMOUNT NEEDED
Yellow	Alize Cotton Gold (Fine/100g - 330m)	2	10g (0.3oz)
Cream	Alize Cotton Gold (Fine/100g - 330m)	67	5g (0.18oz)
Pink	Himalaya Super Lux (DK Light/100g - 250m)	73442	20g (0.7g)
Dark Grey	Gazzal Baby Cotton (Fine/50g - 165m)	3450	10g (0.3oz)
Grey	YarnArt Jeans (Fine/50g - 160m)	80	25g (0.8oz)
Blue	Hello (Fine/25g - 62,5m)	136	10g (0.3oz)

YARN CHART - HOUSE 2			
COLOUR	BRAND/COMPONY	CODE	AMOUNT NEEDED
Yellow	Alize Cotton Gold (Fine/100g - 330m)	2	25g (0.8oz)
Cream	Alize Cotton Gold (Fine/100g - 330m)	67	5g (0.18oz)
Brown	Hello Cotton (Fine/25g - 62,5m)	126	10g (0.3oz)
Tile Red	Hello Cotton (Fine/25g - 62,5m)	117	15g (0.5oz)
Blue	Hello Cotton (Fine/25g - 62,5m)	136	15g (0.5oz)

EMBROIDERY

1 Using a staple gun, stretch the embroidery linen over the wooden frame (see page 20). A frame with the inside dimensions of 20cm (8in) square will give you enough space to work comfortably and keep the amount of fabric used to a minimum. You could work both houses together on one piece of fabric, stretched on a larger frame but there would be some fabric wastage.

2 Place your design template under the frame, hold it up to a light source and trace the pattern that appears on the fabric with a pencil. Adjust your needle to 7.

3 In this project, I wanted the flat side rather than the fluffy one to be the right side, so that the fluffy part could remain inside the holder and serve as the wadding. That's why I decided to use the the brick method of stitching (see page 28). In this technique, we punch our needle in the middle of the stitch in the previous line.

4 You can start your embroidery by filling in the roof part. For House 2, thread your needle with cream yarn.

5 To create the effect of a tiled roof, embroider all the lines in cream first. Before changing to a different colour, use the cream to embroider the outline of the door and windows Keep the setting of your needle at 7 throughout this project.

6 After completing the lines, thread your needle with tile red yarn and fill in the tile shapes on the roof one by one. Rather than filling in the shapes by following the outline and working inwards, work in horizontal rows, using the brick method of stitching. When you have filled one brick, cut your yarn then move on to filling the next one. Resist the temptation to continue without cutting the yarn because this increases the chance of the stitches coming out.

7 After completing the roof, thread your needle with blue yarn and fill in the windows, working in horizontal rows and using brick method as before.

8 When the windows are done, use the same technique to fill in the door with brown yarn.

9 After all the details are finished, thread your needle with yellow yarn and fill in the rest of the house. Punch the needle in rows and using the brick method but work vertically rather than horizontally.

10 Embroider House 1 in the same way: work the cream lines first, then fill in the windows, door and roof in the same way as for House 2. Finish by working the rest of the house in vertical rows.

11 Remove your fabric from the frame using a staple remover or screwdriver and pliers. I do not recommend applying glue to the back of this project. The glue will harden a little after it dries and the pot holder will be a bit stiff. Since we designed this project as a pot holder, it should be flexible. The risk of the embroidery stitches coming out is very low as we will cover the back anyway.

NOTE

If you want to use this project as a trivet or a holder, it is recommended to use only cotton threads for safety.

MAKING UP THE POT HOLDER

1 After removing your project from the frame, trim the fabric to 3cm (1¼in) all round. Plug in your hot glue gun and wait for it to warm up.

2 Lay your embroidered piece out flat, right side down. Use the glue gun to apply glue around the margin of fabric around the edges, then fold it in, towards the fluffy side. Try to do this as tightly as possible because we don't want the fabric to be visible on the right side.

3 After turning under the edges of the embroidered piece, use the design template to cut out another house shape from your backing fabric. If you are using felt, you can cut it out exactly the same shape as the template. if you are using a fabric that can fray, cut this out with a 2cm (¾in) allowance all round, then turn this allowance to the wrong side all round and press.

4 Thread your sewing needle and tie a knot at the end. Bring the embroidered piece and the backing fabric wrong sides together, so the fluffy side of the work is inside, and sew along the sides of the walls and along the base, taking small stitches – leave the roof section unstitched.

5 Fold one leather strip in half. Insert it between the embroidery and the backing at the position of a chimney; stitch it to the backing fabric. Continue to sew the embroidery and backing fabric together around the roof section, stitching through the strap.

TOTE BAG

In this project, I wanted to give the flowers a 3D look by exploiting the fact that punch needle embroidery has two sides – a flat and a fluffy one. The finished bag is very suitable for both daily use or shopping. I've given it leather straps but you could use different handles, such as wood or wicker, if liked. The bag has been lined, which protects the stitching, and it will keep its shape thanks to the rigidity that we get through punch needle embroidery.

Finished Size: 27 x 35cm (10¾ x 14in)

MATERIALS & TOOLS

» Embroidery linen, 45 x 50cm (18 x 20in)
» Wooden frame, 35 x 40cm (14 x 16in)
» Adjustable punch needle
» Yarn – DK/Light Worsted and 4 ply/ Sport weight, *see Chart right for suggestions, colours and amounts*
» Two leather straps, each 2.5cm (1in) wide and 80cm (32in) long
» Sewing machine
» Sewing needle and thread
» Scissors
» Canvas fabric for the back of the bag, 40 x 45cm (16 x 18in)
» Staple gun
» Staple remover or screwdriver and pliers
» Pencil
» Design template - sheet 1A
» Fabric glue (optional)
» Fabric for lining, 75 x 85cm (30 x 34in)

YARN CHART			
COLOUR	BRAND/COMPONY	CODE	AMOUNT NEEDED
Khaki	Alize Cotton Gold (Fine/100g - 330m)	270	100g (3.5oz)
Yellow	Alize Cotton Gold (Fine/100g - 330m)	2	25g (0.8oz)
White	Hello Cotton (Fine/25g - 62,5m)	155	25g (0.8oz)

EMBROIDERY

1 Stretch your fabric onto the frame using a staple gun (see page 20). The more taut your fabric, the easier it will be to punch the needle. A 35 x 40cm (14 x 16in) frame will be large enough for you to work comfortably.

2 Transfer the design template to your fabric (see page 22). Alternatively, draw random 2cm (¾in) diameter circles over the fabric. Draw some semi-circles at the edges of the design area.

3 Adjust your punch needle to 5 and thread it with yellow yarn (see page 22).

4 Fill in the circles by embroidering the outline first and then continuing to fill them in with concentric circles. Work the circles close enough together so the fabric between cannot be seen.

5 After completing the circles, adjust your needle to 12 and thread it with white yarn.

6 Embroider two rings of white yarn around the yellow circles. Because you have increased the length of your needle, the white sections will have longer loops and will look like the petals of a flower.

7 When you have finished the flowers, turn your frame over. Adjust your punch needle back to 5, then thread it with the khaki yarn.

8 Working in horizontal rows, fill in the space around the flowers using the brick method (see page 28).

9 When your embroidery is finished, you can apply fabric glue to the wrong side, leaving it to dry for 24 hours. However, as the bag is lined the use of glue is optional.

10 Remove your finished work from the frame using a staple remover or a screwdriver and pliers. Trim the edges of fabric, leaving an allowance of at least 3cm (1¼in) all round.

MAKING UP THE TOTE BAG

1 Lay the finished embroidery out flat, right side up. Cut out a piece of canvas for the back panel of your bag, leaving a margin of at least 3cm (1¼in) all round for a seam allowance. This may sound like quite a large allowance, but embroidery linens fray easily so it is always better to have a bit extra at the seams.

2 Place the embroidered work and back panel right sides together and pin around the sides and bottom edge. Sew around the pinned edges as close to the embroidered stitching as possible. Trim off any excess fabric around the edges and snip across the corners to reduce bulk. If liked, stabilise the seam by adding zigzag stitching all round or by brushing on some fabric glue. Turn your bag right side out.

3 For the lining, cut our two more pieces of canvas, including a 3cm (1¼in) seam allowance. Sew the two lining pieces right sides together and pin around the sides and bottom edge. Sew around the pinned edges, leaving a 12cm (4¾in) gap in one of the sides; you will use this gap later on to turn the bag to the right side.

4 With the lining still wrong side out, place the outer part of your bag inside the lining. Sew the upper edges of the lining and bag together, stitching as as close to the embroidered stitching as possible.

5 Turn your bag right side out by gently pulling it through the 12cm (4¾in) gap you left in the side. Push the lining inside the bag. Poke a finger into the corners to make your bag a neat rectangle shape.

6 Sew the leather straps to your bag with a sewing needle and thread. To make them more secure, you can use the type of waxed thread that is generally used in leather work.

BUTTERFLY RUG

One of the things about punch needle embroidery that I like the best is how you can create projects in different scales: it's possible to make a tiny hair clip or a big rug by using the same needle. In this project, I wanted to embroider something larger and so designed a butterfly-shaped rug for my daughter's room. All you need is a bigger frame and a little more time.

MATERIALS & TOOLS

» Monk's cloth, 110cm (43in) square
» Wooden frame, 100cm (39in) square
» Oxford punch needle no. 10
» Yarn – Chunky/Bulky weight, *see Chart right for suggestions, colours and amounts*
» Scissors
» Staple gun
» Staple remover or screwdriver and pliers
» Pencil
» Design template - sheet 2B
» Fabric glue
» Brush
» Hot glue gun and silicone
» Canvas or iron-on interfacing for backing
» Masking tape

YARN CHART			
COLOUR	BRAND / COMPANY	CODE	AMOUNT NEEDED
Cream	Kartopu Punto (Bulky/100g - 110m)	K025	250g (8.8oz)
Pink	Kartopu Punto (Bulky/100g - 110m)	M2057	75g (2.6oz)
Black	Kartopu Punto (Bulky/100g - 110m)	K940	100g (3.5oz)
Orange	Myboshi (Bulky/50g - 42m)	173	100g (3.5oz)
Green	Kartopu Cozy Wool (Bulky/100g - 110m)	M448	50g (1.75oz)
Yellow	Kartopu Punto (Bulky/100g - 110m)	M1037	100g (3.5oz)
Purple	Kartopu Punto (Bulky/100g - 110m)	M3008	50g (1.75oz)
Blue	Kartopu Punto (Bulky/100g - 110m)	M8007	60g (2.1oz)

EMBROIDERY

1 For this rug, we will be working with a 1m (39in) square frame. You will find it very difficult to embroider on a frame of this size while holding onto it, so a frame with some kind of support that allows you to sit or stand in front of it will be the best choice. Stretch your fabric onto the frame with the help of a staple gun, making sure that the fabric is as taut as possible.

2 Place your butterfly design template under the frame, taping it down around the edges if liked. Hold up the frame to a light source so you can see the design through the fabric and trace over it with a pencil (see page 21).

3 After transferring the design to the fabric, thread your punch needle with black yarn. For this project, I preferred using the Oxford no. 10 needle. You can start by filling in two circle shapes on the wings. Remember to pull the start of your yarn to the underside of the fabric with your hand when you insert your needle for the first time. Embroider the outline of the circles and then fill in them.

4 You can continue with those other parts you need to embroider with black yarn, such as the lines on the lower wings. Normally, you would pull the start of the yarn to the back to reduce the risk of the embroidery unravelling, but if I'm working on a single line, I usually do not do this. So, in order to have a neater look, keep the starting and finishing ends of yarn on the flat side if you are embroidering a single line.

5 After completing the areas you need to fill in with black yarn, you can continue in any colour, but remember to work shapes within shapes first. Remember to check the fluffy side while you are working because if there is a mistake you can fix it before it is too late.

6 After filling in all the shapes, you can remove your project from the frame using a staple remover or a screwdriver and pliers.

MAKING UP THE RUG

1 After removing your embroidery from the frame, lay it out flat so the fluffy side is facing downwards and trim the fabric around the edges, leaving 6 – 7cm (2¼ – 2¾in) allowance.

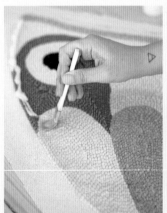 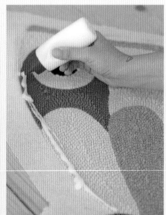

2 Generally speaking, the use of fabric glue on the back of your work is optional for most projects. However, with this project it's essential. As it goes on the floor, this rug can get dirty faster and may need to be cleaned more often than other projects. Therefore, it will be useful to fix the embroidery by brushing the back with fabric glue and leaving to dry for 24 hours.

3 When the fabric glue has dried, snip small notches in the curved edges of the allowance to make it easier to turn them under. Fold the allowance to the wrong side and use a hot glue gun to stick it in place.

4 You can complete the rug by stitching down the turned allowance with a needle and thread. Alternatively, cut out some canvas to the right shape, with a 2 – 3cm (¾ – 1¼in) allowance. Turn under the edge and sew to the wrong side of the rug. You could also use iron-on interfacing for this.

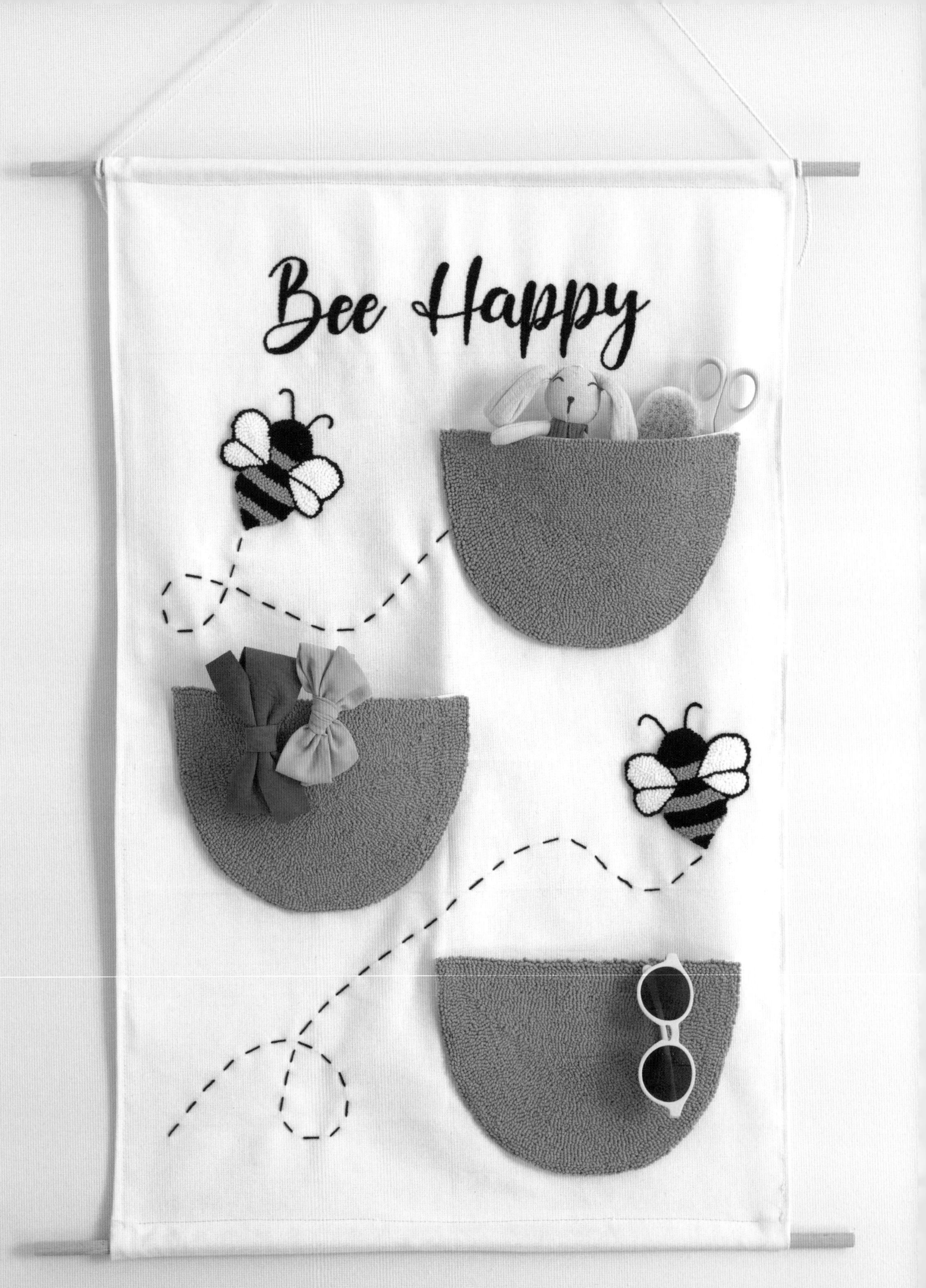
Bee Happy

WALL ORGANISER

An organiser is a great project to make with a punch needle. It's something that allows you easy access to essential items, but at the same time looks decorative and complements your home. In a kid's room in particular, an organiser like this can be a real life saver, helping you to keep items in daily use close to hand. With this in mind, I created a wall organiser decorated with bees that would suit a nursery decor well. The great thing about an organiser is that it can be hung anywhere you like, whether that's on the wall, beside the bed or even inside a cupboard.

Finished Size: 47 x 75cm (18½ x 30in)

MATERIALS & TOOLS

- » Duck linen fabric, 60 x 80cm (24 x 32in), for the base
- » Duck linen fabric, 60cm (24in) square, for the pockets
- » Wooden frame, 50cm (20in) square
- » Embroidery hoop, 25cm (10in)
- » Adjustable punch needle
- » Yarn – DK/Light Worsted and 4 ply/Sport weight, *see Chart right for suggestions, colours and amounts*
- » Scissors
- » Staple gun
- » Staple remover or screwdriver and pliers
- » Pencil
- » Design template - sheet 2A
- » Fabric glue (optional)
- » Two wooden doweling rods, 1.5cm (⅝in) diameter and 60cm (24in) long
- » Cotton cord for hanging, 50cm (20in)
- » Sewing machine
- » Hot glue gun
- » Sewing needle and thread
- » Iron

YARN CHART			
COLOUR	BRAND / COMPANY	CODE	AMOUNT NEEDED
Black	Alize Cotton Gold (Fine/100g - 330m)	60	50g (1.75oz)
Yellow	Alize Cotton Gold (Fine/100g - 330m)	2	100g (3.5oz)
Cream	Alize Cotton Gold (Fine/100g - 330m)	1	25g (0.8oz)

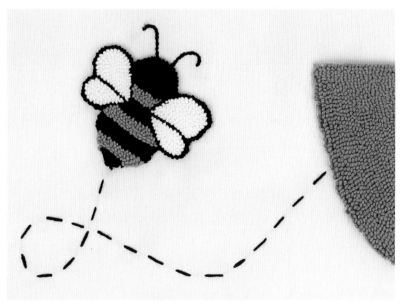

EMBORIDERY

1 This project is worked in two stages. The first is embroidering the sections that will form the pockets; the second is preparing the base onto which the pockets are attached. Since not all of the base fabric is filled in and because it will be seen, I have used duck linen, which has a less open structure.

2 Start by stretching the 60cm (24in) square piece of duck linen onto the wooden frame with a staple gun, making sure the fabric is as taut as possible. Transfer the semi-circular pocket designs onto the fabric. You can place the design template under the frame, and trace over it, or use carbon paper. Leave 5–6cm (2-2¼in) between the semi-circles to fit all three within the frame.

3 After transferring the design to the fabric, adjust your punch needle to 6. Thread it with yellow yarn and fill in each semi circle, remembering to pull the starting point of the yarn through to the underside.

4 When you've embroidered all the pockets, remove the fabric from the frame with a staple remover or a screwdriver and pliers and cut them out, leaving a margin 2–3cm (¾-1¼in) of fabric all round.

5 Transfer the design template to the 60 x 80cm (24 x 32in) piece of fabric that will form the base of the organiser. The 'Bee Happy' motto will be embroidered on the flat side of the work, so you should write this out on the front of the fabric. Because the bees will be formed by the fluffy side of the work, you should turn the fabric over and draw these on the back. You can use carbon paper for drawing, or place the design template under the fabric and trace it with a pencil.

6 Once the design has been transferred, stretch your fabric in the hoop, centring it over one of the bees. Put the inner part the hoop under the fabric and the part with the adjustable screw on top. After stretching the fabric, tighten the screw with a pliers.

7 You can start by embroidering the bee with the yellow yarn that is already in to your punch needle. Keep the setting of the needle at 6.

8 Thread your needle with black yarn and embroider the bee's black stripes, the outline of the wings and the antennae. Remember to pull the starting point of the yarn through to the underside. As the antennae consist of single lines, there is no need to pull the starting thread to the back in this section.

9 Finally, thread your needle with white yarn and fill in the inside of the wings to complete the first bee. Remove your hoop from the fabric and stretch your fabric again, centred over the other bee. Embroider this bee in the same way as the first.

10 After finishing the second bee, remove your fabric from the hoop and turn it over. Since you want the 'Bee Happy' text to be flat and not fluffy, you will work from the front side of the fabric. After centring your hoop over the text, fill it with black yarn.

11 Once you've finished the embroidery, trim the starting and finishing ends yarns so they are even with the loops. If liked, you can brush glue over the side of the work that will not be seen and leave it to dry.

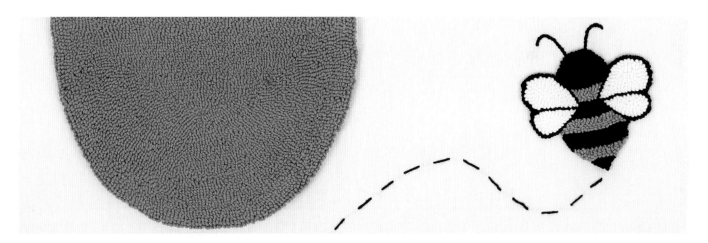

MAKING UP THE ORGANISER

1 Lay the pocket sections out flat with the fluffy parts facing downwards. Snip small notches in the curved edges to make it easier to turn them under. Get your hot glue gun ready.

2 Fold the allowance to the wrong side all round and use a hot glue gun to stick in place. Do this as neatly as possible so that the base fabric cannot be seen on the fluffy side.

3 Take the background piece on which you have embroidered the bees and text and fold under the left and right edges by 1cm (⅜in). Press, then stitch in place using a sewing machine.

4 Turn under the top and bottom edges by 3cm (1¼in). Press, then stitch in place, making sure you leave a 2cm (¾in) wide channel at both edge.

5 Apply fabric glue to the curved edges of the pockets and stick them in place. Once the glue has dried, use a sewing needle and thread and hand stitch neatly around the curved edges to make them more secure.

6 Pass the doweling rods through the channels at the top and bottom of the organiser. Tie the ends of a 50cm (20in) length of cotton cord to either end of the topmost rod to form the hanging loop.

7 Finally, thread your needle with black yarn and tie a knot in one end. Decorate your organiser by working 1cm (⅜in) long running stitches across the background in a line to suggest the flight paths of the bees. If liked, draw these lines in with a pencil before you begin. Complete the project by sewing felt on to the back.

TERRAZZO HAIR CLIP

There's a trend at the moment for decoration that's inspired by Italian terrazzo. In fact, terrazzo is nothing new, its roots go back to the 15th century and to Venice. Terrazzo surfaces, usually for flooring, were made up of small pieces of different materials such as marble, glass, stone or granite, held together with a special mortar to create multi-coloured and unique patterns. I was inspired by these patterns and wanted to make a hair clip that featured the warmth of terrazzo style and turn it into an attractive accessory to wear. Since this is a very small make, I've used embroidery threads as they are finer compared to the yarn I've use in other projects.

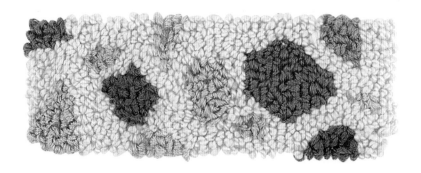

Finished Size: 9 x 3cm (3½ x 1¼in)

MATERIALS & TOOLS

» Duck linen, 20cm (8in) square
» Embroidery hoop, 15cm (6in)
» Adjustable punch needle
» DMC embroidery thread – *see Chart right for colours and amounts*
» Scissors
» Pen
» Design template - sheet 1B
» Fabric glue (optional)
» Hair clip attachment
» Hot glue gun and silicone
» Sewing needle and thread

YARN CHART			
COLOUR	BRAND/COMPANY	CODE	AMOUNT NEEDED
Ecru	DMC Embroidery Thread (Super Fine/8m)	117	2 skeins
Tile Red	DMC Embroidery Thread (Super Fine/8m)	920	1 skein
Blue	DMC Embroidery Thread (Super Fine/8m)	797	1 skein
Green	DMC Embroidery Thread (Super Fine/8m)	964	1 skein
Yellow	DMC Embroidery Thread (Super Fine/8m)	676	1 skein
Pink	DMC Embroidery Thread (Super Fine/8m)	224	1 skein

EMBROIDERY

1 Stretch your fabric in your embroidery hoop. If you are using a wooden hoop, wrap a strip of fabric around the inner piece of your hoop to help your embroidery fabric grip the surface of the hoop and stay in place.

2 Transfer the design to the fabric by using carbon paper or by placing it under the hoop and tracing over the design.

3 Adjust your needle to 6. Because I chose fine thread for this project, I used duck linen as the fabric, as it has a tighter weave compared to other embroidery linens. Do not separate the strands of the embroidery thread for this project; use all six strands together.

4 Start by filling in the coloured shapes that make up the terrazzo pattern. Pull the starting point of the thread to the underside when you first insert your needle in the fabric.

5 After you have embroidered all the small shapes, thread your needle with the ecru colour first, embroider around the edge of the hair clip and then fill in all the gaps around the coloured shapes.

6 After completing the embroidery, trim the starting and finishing ends of threads so they are even with the loops of the fluffy part. Trim the edges of the fabric, leaving a margin of 2 – 3cm (¾ – 1¼in) all round.

MAKING UP THE HAIR CLIP

1 Lay your finished piece out flat with the fluffy part facing downwards. Fold the 2 – 3cm (¾ – 1¼in) allowance towards the inside and stick in place using a hot glue gun.

2 Thread your sewing needle and tie a knot in the end of the thread. Sew the hair clip attachment to the underside of your finished piece. I would not recommend sticking the metal hair clip in place with the hot glue gun because the silicone will not provide an effective bond.

BOOK COVER

I always carry a notebook with me so I can jot down any new ideas that pop into my head and make lists of all the things I need to do. I also carry any books that I'm reading so that I can read a few pages during spare moments. Until a few years ago, I would just shove my books and notebook in my bag only to find them getting damaged. I solved this problem by sewing myself some covers. Once I started embroidering with a punch needle, I realised that my new craft was ideal for making book covers so I designed this one. You can personalise your books and notebooks in the same way and protect them at the same time.

Finished Size: 17 x 23cm (16¼ x 9in) when closed

MATERIALS & TOOLS

» Embroidery linen, 50cm (20in) square
» Wooden frame, 40cm (16in) square
» Adjustable punch needle
» Yarn – DK/Light Worsted and 4 ply/
  Sport weight, *see Chart right for
  suggestions, colours and amounts*
» Scissors
» Staple gun
» Staple remover or screwdriver and
  pliers
» Design template - sheet 1B
» Fabric glue (optional)
» Fabric for lining, 60cm (24in) square
» Two leather straps, each 2.5cm (1in)
  wide and 14cm (5½in) long
» Sewing needle and thread

YARN CHART			
COLOUR	BRAND/COMPANY	CODE	AMOUNT NEEDED
Yellow	La Mia Cottony (DK Light/50g - 120m)	P15-L015	25g (0.8oz)
Red	La Mia Cottony (DK Light/50g - 120m)	P11-L011	25g (0.8oz)
Black	Alize Cotton Gold (Fine/100g - 330m)	60	25g (0.8oz)
Orange	HELLO Cotton (Fine/25g - 62,5m)	118	25g (0.8oz)
White	Alize Cotton Gold (Fine/100g - 330m)	55	100g (3.5oz)
Pink	HELLO Cotton (Fine/25g - 62,5m)	111	25g (0.8oz)
Dark Blue	Alize Cotton Gold (Fine/100g - 330m)	279	25g (0.8oz)
Blue	HELLO Cotton (Fine/25g - 62,5m)	136	25g (0.8oz)
Green	HELLO Cotton (Fine/25g - 62,5m)	137	25g (0.8oz)

EMBROIDERY

1 Using a staple gun, stretch your fabric onto the frame. It is very important to stretch the fabric evenly so you can punch your needle easily. You can gently pull your fabric from the edges while stapling it to make it more taut. (see page 20).

2 Place your design template under the frame. Hold up the frame to a light source so you can see the design through the fabric and trace over it with a pencil. If you look at the template, you will see that the 'hi!' is flipped horizontally. If the underside of a piece of punch needle embroidery – the fluffy part – is going to be the right side, any lettering or numbers need to be transferred to the fabric in this way to get the right result. I call this the mirror effect (see page 21).

3 Since the shapes on this book cover are all separate you can start with which one you wish. Adjust your needle to 5 and thread it with the yarn that's needed for your starting shape.

4 First, embroider the outline of the shape and be careful to follow this outline while filling it in. For example, if you are filling in a triangle, aim to fill it by making small triangles, rather than working back and forth in rows.

5 Keep the needle setting at 5 and embroider all the shapes one by one before filling in the 'hi!'. Thread your punch needle with white yarn and fill in the space between the shapes. While embroidering the background, you can work in rows, so that you have a smooth look and it will be easier to embroider the areas between the shapes.

6 Once you've filled in the background, trim any starting and finishing ends of yarns to the same length as the stitch loops and remove your project from the frame.

7 As this project is lined, it's not essential to use glue to secure the embroidery. However, you can if liked; remember to leave until completely dry.

MAKING UP THE BOOK COVER

1 After removing your project from the frame, lay it out flat with the fluffy part facing downwards. Trim the edges of the fabric, leaving a margin of 2cm (¾in) all round.

2 Cut out two pieces of lining fabric, each 23 x 12cm (9 x 4¾in), for the pockets. Turn under one long edge on each piece and press in place. Using a sewing machine, stitch along the turnings.

3 Cut out a 23 x 30cm (9 x 12in) piece of lining fabric and lay it out flat, right side up. Place the two pocket pieces on top, right side down. Pin around the edges of the pocket pieces, leaving the hemmed edge unpinned; sew in place.

4 Lay the finished embroidery out flat, fluffy side up. Fold one strap in half and place the ends on one short side edge so they line up with the edge of the fabric and the loop of the strap points towards the centre. Position the strap ends about 6cm (2¼in) apart. Using a needle and thread, stitch the strap ends to the fabric allowance. Repeat to stitch the other strap to the other side of the finished embroidery.

5 Lay the finished embroidery out flat again, right side up, and place the lining on top, right side down. Pin all round the edges.

6 Sew all round the edges, leaving a 10cm (4in) gap along the bottom (you will use this gap later to turn the cover to the right side). Do not attempt to stitch through the straps as your sewing machine is unlikely to be able to sew through the leather; simply stop stitching when you get to these.

7 Turn your cover to the right side through the gap in the bottom edge. Thread your sewing needle and tie a knot at the end of the thread. Neatly hand stitch the gap closed.

8 To use your cover, slip the cover of your book and notebook into the pockets.

GARLAND

I started punch needle embroidery by making bags for my daughter and cushions for her room, and these played a big part in turning my hobby into my passion. Therefore, any projects I make for children will always be special to me. As time went by, I felt the need to diversify the things I was making with my punch needle and so I added projects such as garlands and banners to my list. For this project, I've created a garland worked in natural tones and completed with wooden beads that would suit either boys' or girls' bedrooms.

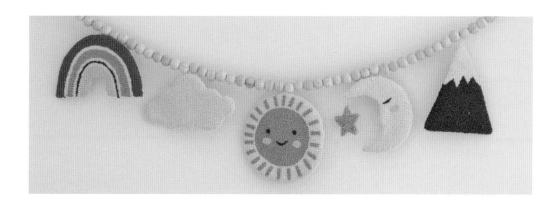

MATERIALS & TOOLS

» Embroidery linen, 60cm (24in) square
» Wooden frame, 50cm (20in) square)
» Adjustable punch needle
» Yarn – DK/Light Worsted and 4 ply/ Sport weight, *see Chart right for suggestions, colours and amounts*
» Scissors
» Staple gun
» Staple remover or screwdriver and pliers
» Pencil
» Design template - pages 123–124
» Fabric glue (optional)
» Hot glue gun and silicone
» 8–10mm (¼–⅜in) wooden beads x 60
» Cotton cord, 120cm
» Felt for backing

YARN CHART			
COLOUR	BRAND / COMPANY	CODE	AMOUNT NEEDED
Pink	Alize Cotton Gold (Fine/100g - 330m)	393	10g (0.3oz)
Yellow	Alize Cotton Gold (Fine/100g - 330m)	2	25g (0.8oz)
Cream	Alize Cotton Gold (Fine/100g - 330m)	1	50g (1.75oz)
Coal Grey	La Mia Cottony (DK Light/50g - 120m)	P19	15g (0.5oz)
Tile Red	Nako Pırlanta (DK Light/100g - 225m)	11252	25g (0.8oz)
Gold	Diva Lurex (Super Fine/25g -160m)	1	10g (0.3oz)

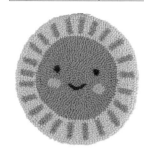
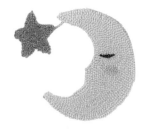

Finished Size: 90cm (35½in) long

EMBROIDERY

1 Stretch your fabric onto the frame with a staple gun (see page 20). It is very important that your fabric is as taut as possible so that you can punch your needle easily.

2 This garland consists of five separate pieces and it is possible to fit all five into a 50 x 50cm (20 x 20in) frame. Place the design templates under the frame, hold it up to a light source and trace over the images (see page 21). Leave at least a 4cm (11/2in) space between the shapes because when the embroidery is finished, we will cut them out separately.

3 Adjust your punch needle to 5 and thread it with coal grey yarn. You can adjust your needle to a number higher than 5 if you wish, but bear in mind that a higher setting will mean you need more yarn and that the loops will have a greater tendency to tangle. So, if you want a tighter look to the fluffy part, 5 or 6 will be the ideal setting.

4 Using the coal grey yarn, fill in the mouth and eyes on the sun, the eye on the moon, the single line on the rainbow and the bottom of the mountain. Remember to pull the yarn to the back when you start the embroidery. When you embroider a single line, you can punch your needle more closely to make smaller stitches than usual.

5 Thread your punch needle with the pink yarn and use it to fill in the cheeks on both the moon and the sun and the pink section on the rainbow.

6 Thread your punch needle with cream and complete the top of the mountain, the background of the moon, the entire cloud and the cream sections on the rainbow. We will embroider the cream parts of the sun after embroidering the yellow parts because we need to fill the inner sections before completing the background.

7 Using the other colours, continue to fill in the shapes in any order you wish.

8 Once you've filled in all the shapes, flip your frame over and trim the starting and finishing yarns to a length that's even with the loops.

9 When your embroidery is finished, you can apply glue to the wrong side if liked, leaving it to dry for 24 hours. However, as the shapes will be backed with felt this stage is not essential.

10 Remove your fabric from the frame using a staple remover or a screwdriver and pliers. Cut out the shapes, leaving 2–3cm (¾–1¼in) allowance around each one.

MAKING UP THE GARLAND

1 After removing your project from the frame, lay the shapes out flat with the fluffy parts facing downwards. Snip small notches into the curved edges of the allowance of each shape to make it easier to turn them. In the meantime, you can get your hot glue gun ready. You can also use fabric glue in this project but I prefer the silicone of the hot glue gun because it dries much faster than many other adhesives.

2 Using the glue gun, apply adhesive to the notched edges and fold them to the flat side of your embroidery, pressing down to secure. Try to do this neatly so that the fabric cannot be seen on the fluffy side.

3 Using the design templates, cut out the same shapes from felt. Using a needle and thread, sew the felt backing pieces to the embroidered shapes, inserting a short loop of cord at the top of each one. You will use these loops to hang the shapes onto the cord and form the garland.

4 When you've backed all the shapes, string ten wooden beads onto your long piece of cord, then add one of the shapes. Follow this with ten more beads and another shape. Continue in this way to string all the beads and shapes onto the cord in any order you wish.

5 Knot the ends of the cord together and then hang it in your desired position.

FLORAL EMBOSSED CUSHION

Cushions are among the most popular items used in home decoration and I especially like that they are practical as well as decorative. From the living room to the bedroom, they can be used in all areas of your house. In this project, I tried to create a modern cushion by combining floral patterns with a few small geometric shapes. I made the flowers look embossed by leaving the background of the design unstitched. This cushion will add colour to your home and brighten up your sofa when you're relaxing.

Finished Size: 37 x 37cm(14½ x 14½in)

MATERIALS & TOOLS

» Duck canvas, 50cm (20in) square
» Wooden frame, 40cm (16in) square
» Adjustable punch needle
» Yarn – DK/Light Worsted and 4 ply/ Sport weight, *see Chart right for suggestions, colours and amounts*
» Scissors
» Staple gun
» Staple remover or screwdriver and pliers
» Pencil
» Design template - sheet 1A
» Fabric glue (optional)
» Zip, 40cm (16in)
» Canvas fabric for backing, 45cm (18in) square
» Sewing machine
» Iron

YARN CHART			
COLOUR	BRAND / COMPANY	CODE	AMOUNT NEEDED
Yellow	Alize Cotton Gold (Fine/100g - 330m)	2	30g (1oz)
Cream	Alize Cotton Gold (Fine/100g - 330m)	67	30g (1oz)
Navy Blue	Yarnart Jeans (Fine/50g - 160m)	54	50g (1.75oz)
Tile Red	Nako Pırlanta (DK Light/100g - 225m)	11252	30g (1oz)
Beige	La mia Cottony (Fine/100g - 330m)	P4 L004	15g (0.5oz)

EMBROIDERY

1 Stretch your fabric onto the frame with the help of the staple gun (see page 20). Since the background of this design is not filled in, I've chosen to use duck canvas which has a less open weave when compared to other embroidery linens. I should point out that, although the weave is tighter, this fabric is as suitable as other embroidery linens. A frame with an inner width of 40 x 40cm (16 x 16in) will give you enough space to work comfortably.

2 Place your design template under the frame and hold it up to a light source so you can see the design through the fabric; trace over it with a pencil (see page 21).

3 Adjust your needle to 5 (keep at this setting for the whole project). Because the background is not filled in the flowers will stand out against the fabric background and we can get the fluffy look we want on as low a setting as 5.

4 Since the flowers and leaves in the pattern are not linked to each other, you can start with whichever one you want. But don't forget, if there are shapes within shapes, you must start with the innermost shape. For example, we must embroider the middle of a flower first and then fill in the petals.

You can punch your needle a little closer while embroidering single lines (such as a flower stalk) so that there is no gap between the loops and the fabric cannot be seen between the lines.

5 Thread your punch needle with the yarn you need for wherever you wish to start, then fill in that shape. Once you've filled each shape, cut your yarn and start afresh on the next shape. In punch needle embroidery, I do not recommend that you skip from one shape to another one without cutting the yarn as this increases the risk of your stitches coming out.

6 Once you have finished embroidering the flowers and shapes, trim any starting and finishing lengths of yarn so they are even with the fluffy part.

7 Remove your finished project from the frame using a staple remover or a screwdriver and pliers. Trim the edges of fabric, leaving an allowance of at least 3cm (1¼in) all round.

8 Because the background of this cushion is not filled in, it is not as tightly stitched as other projects, so I recommend that you brush fabric glue on the flat side of the work. Leave it to dry for 24 hours.

MAKING UP THE CUSHION

1 Cut out a piece of backing fabric that is 3cm (1¼in) wider than the finished piece of embroidery.

2 You can add a zip to the bottom of the pillow, but I prefer to sew it in the centre of the backing. To do this, fold your backing fabric in half and cut along the fold. Turn under the long edges of these both pieces by about 1cm (⅜in) and press. Open your zip and pin one side of it to the pressed edge of one fabric piece. Using a sewing machine, stitch it in place.

3 Pin the other side of the zip to the pressed edge of the other fabric piece, then stitch in place. Close the zip so the backing is one piece.

4 Lay the embroidered piece out flat, right side up and place the backing on top, right side down. Open the zip by about 10cm (4in), then pin the two pieces together. Sew all round, stitching as close to the embroidery as possible.

5 When you have finished sewing, trim off any excess fabric around the edges and snip across the corners to reduce bulk. If liked, you can stabilise the seam by adding zigzag stitching all round or by brushing on some fabric glue. Open the zip completely and turn the cushion cover to the right side through the gap. Push your finger into the corners to shape the cover into a square.

LAMPSHADE

You can use punch needle embroidery to make things from scratch and to upcycle existing items. I think this project is a great example of a renovation idea: I wanted to give a lampshade a new look by covering it with an embossed piece of embroidery. I've chosen ethnic-inspired patterns for this project and I've used a single colour to achieve a simple elegance.

Finished Size: Diameter and height of 15cm (6in)

MATERIALS & TOOLS

» Duck linen, 60 x 25cm (24 x 10in)
» Wooden frame, 55 x 20cm (21½ x 8in)
» Adjustable punch needle
» Lampshade with a diameter and height of 15cm (6in)
» Yarn – DK/Light Worsted and 4 ply/ Sport weight, *see Chart right for suggestion, colour and amount*
» Scissors
» Staple gun
» Staple remover or screwdriver and pliers
» Pencil
» Design template - sheet 2A
» Fabric glue (optional)
» Hot glue gun and silicone

YARN CHART			
COLOUR	BRAND / COMPANY	CODE	AMOUNT NEEDED
Cream	Alize Cotton Gold (Fine/100g - 330m)	67	50g (1.75oz)

EMBROIDERY

1 Using a staple gun, stretch your fabric onto the frame (see page 20). Since the background of this design is not embroidered, I've used duck linen which has a less open weave. After measuring the dimensions of my own lampshade, I decided that a frame with an interior width of 55 x 20cm (21½ x 8in) would be suitable. However, these dimensions may vary depending on the lampshade you use.

2 Place your design template under the frame, hold it up to the light and use a pencil to trace the image that appears on the front. If you wish, you can use carbon paper: place your fabric-covered frame on the table and put your design template on top. Slip the carbon paper between them and go over all the design with a pencil to transfer the image to the fabric (see page 21).)

3 Adjust your punch needle to 5 and keep it at this setting. Because we will not fill in the background, we can get the embossed look we want even with a low setting like 5, and we can also keep the yarn usage to a minimum.

4 Thread your needle with cream yarn. You can start from any point you want since the shapes are all separate from each other. First embroider the outlines of the shapes, then fill them in. When you've finished each shape, cut your yarn before starting on the next shape. In punch needle embroidery, I do not recommend jumping from one shape to another without cutting the yarn as it increases the risk of unravelling.

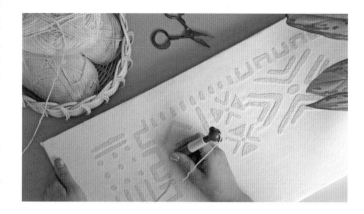

5 When all the shapes have been worked, trim the ends of the starting and finishing yarns neatly. Remove your project from the frame using a staple remover or a screwdriver and pliers. Trim the edges of fabric, leaving an allowance of at least 3cm (1¼in) all round.

6 As this is not an item that will be washed, I did not use fabric glue on the back. You can clean the lampshade by wiping it with a damp cloth. If you do apply glue to the back, leave it to dry for 24 hours.

MAKING UP THE LAMPSHADE

1 Lay your finished embroidery out flat with the fluffy part facing downwards. Meanwhile, you can set your hot glue gun to warm up..

2 Place your lampshade over the fabric. Spread glue along the allowances on the long edges of your finished piece. Roll the embroidered fabric around the lampshade, tucking the glued edges inside the top and bottom.

3 Turn under one short edge and lap this one over the other; glue in place.

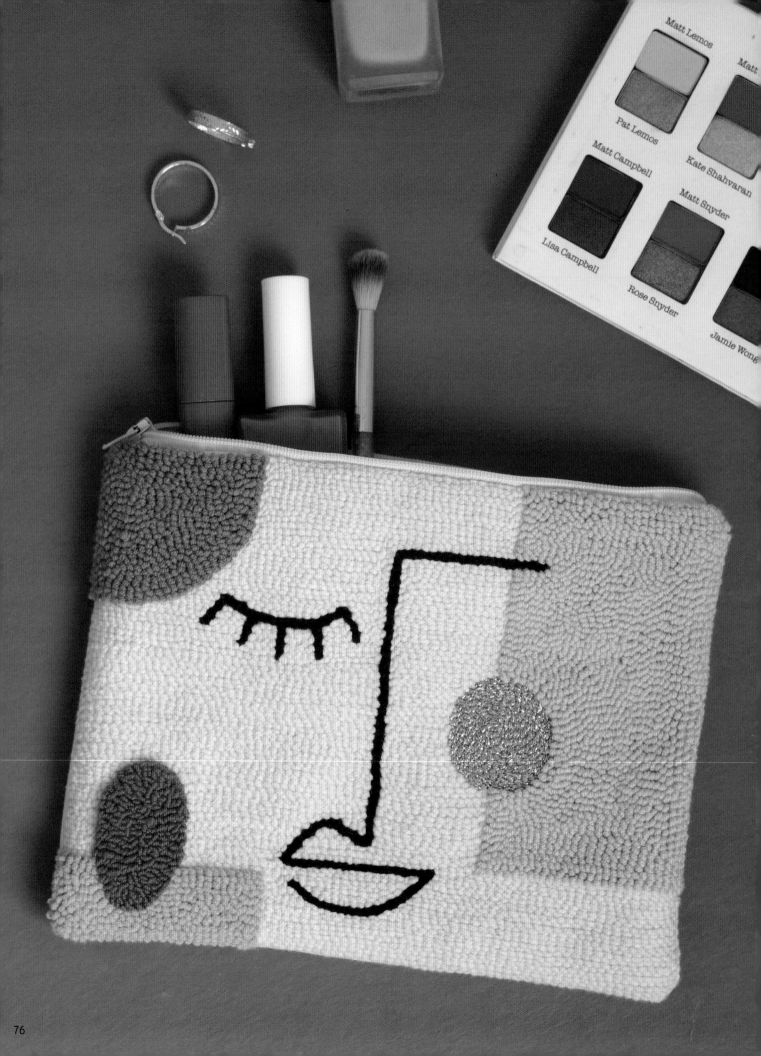

MAKE-UP BAG

A recent trend that you can see in many different fields such as decoration and textiles, is the artistic technique known 'one line'. Sometimes called 'one line art' or 'minimalist drawing', this is a technique based on drawing without taking your hand off the page and letting your imagination do the rest. I got interested in this art form after attending workshop and thought that I could integrate it into some of my punch needle work to add a modern touch. In this project, I've created a make-up bag, decorated with a minimal face design, that you can keep in your handbag.

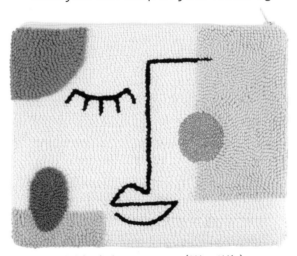

Finished Size: 21 x 16cm (8¼ x 6¼in)

MATERIALS & TOOLS
» Embrodiery linen 30 x 40cm (12 x 16in)
» Wooden frame, 25 x 35cm (10 x 14in))
» Adjustable Punch needle
» Yarn – DK/Light Worsted and 4 ply/Sport weight, *see Chart right for suggestions, colours and amounts*
» Sewing machine
» Sewing needle and thread
» Scissors
» Canvas fabric for backing, 25 x 35cm (10 x 14in)
» Staple gun and stapler
» Staple remover or screwdriver and pliers
» Pencil
» Design template - page 125
» Fabric glue (optional)
» Zip
» Fabric for lining 50 x 70cm (20 x 27½in)

YARN CHART			
COLOUR	BRAND/COMPANY	CODE	AMOUNT NEEDED
Pink	Alize Cotton Gold (Fine/100g - 330m)	393	15g (0.5oz)
Brown	Yarnart Jeans (Fine/50g - 160m)	71	10g (0.3oz)
Beige	Alize Cotton Gold (Fine/100g - 330m)	67	10g (0.3oz)
Cream	Alize Cotton Gold (Fine/100g - 330m)	1	40g (1.4oz)
Black	Alize Cotton Gold (Fine/100g - 330m)	60	10g (0.3oz)
Gold	Diva Lurex (Super Fine/25g - 160m)	1	10g (0.3oz)
Tile Red	Gazzal Baby Cotton (Fine/50g - 165m)	3454	10g (0.3oz)

EMBROIDERY

1 Stretch your fabric onto the frame with the staple gun. A 35 x 40cm (14 x 16in) frame will be big enough for this rectangular make-up bag. You can easily staple your fabric to your wooden frame if you cut it so you have an extra 5cm (2in) extra on each edge.

2 Place your design template under the frame, hold it up to the light and trace over the image with a pencil to transfer it to the fabric. In this project, you will use both the flat and fluffy parts of our embroidery, so you will embroider some areas from the front of the frame and some parts from the back. Therefore, after transferring the template to the fabric, flip your frame over and draw the shapes on the underside as well.

3 Adjust your punch needle to 6 and thread it with black yarn. Embroider the lines that make up the face in two rows. When you begin, be sure to pull the start of the yarn to the underside with your hand.

4 Thread the punch needle with the gold-coloured lurex yarn and fill in the circle shape. Embroider the outline first then fill in with concentric circles.

5 After completing the circle, turn your frame over and start embroidering all the remaining sections except the cream background. Because these areas will be raised, and have an embossed look, the fluffy part of the stitches needs to be on the right side. Continue to keep your needle setting at 6 throughout this project.

6 When you've finished the embossed sections, turn the frame back over and thread your needle with cream yarn and fill in all the background. As the flat side of the stitches is the right side in this section, you can also use the brick method (see page 23).

7 After filling in all the background, trim the ends of the starting and finishing yarns neatly.

8 When your embroidery is finished, you can apply fabric glue to the side you will not use and leave it to dry for 24 hours. However, as this bag is lined the risk of the work unravelling is low, so using glue for this project is not a must.

9 Remove your finished project from the frame using a staple remover or a screwdriver and pliers. Trim the edges of fabric, leaving an allowance of at least 3cm (1¼in) all round.

MAKING UP THE MAKE-UP BAG

1 Lay out the finished embroidery flat with the right side up. Place the fabric for the back of the bag on top, right side down, and trim to the same size.

2 Open your zip and pin one edge to the top edge of your embroidered piece. Using your sewing machine, sew this in place. Pin the other edge of the zip to the top edge of the back panel; sew in place.

3 Pin the embroidered piece and the back panel right sides together, keeping the zip open and with a gap of at least 10cm (4in). Sew around the sides and bottom edge. Trim off any excess fabric around the edges and snip across the corners to reduce bulk. If liked, you can stabilise the seam by adding zigzag stitching all round or by brushing on some fabric glue. Turn your bag to the right side through the open zip. Push your finger into the corners to shape the bag into a neat rectangle.

4 Cut out two pieces of fabric for the lining of your bag; make each piece the size of the bag plus 2cm (¾in) for a seam allowance. Pin the pieces of fabric right sides together and sew around the sides and bottom edge. After completing the sewing, turn the upper edge of the lining to the wrong side by 2cm (¾in) and press in place.

5 Place the lining inside the bag, wrong side to wrong side. Using a needle and thread, stitch the folded edge of the lining to the bag just under the zip.

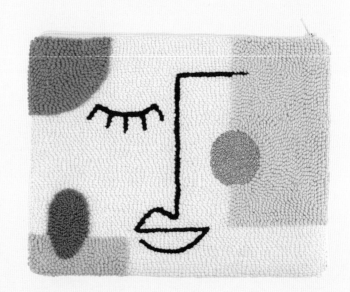

CUTE STUFFED CAT

I've been interested in handmade crafts for many years and if you were to ask me what I enjoy making the most, I would say without hesitation that it's presents for other people. I believe that gifts with a sentimental value are more significant, therefore I try to make special handmade presents for my loved ones rather than buying things. I think this is a great project if, like me, you want to make a present for someone. You can make a cute, soft toy for your own kids or for friends and family. With this project, I was inspired by my own daughter, who loves cats a lot and decided to make a toy version.

Finished Size: 18 x 33cm (7 x 13in)

MATERIALS & TOOLS

» Monk's cloth, 50cm (20in) square
» Wooden frame, 40cm (16in) square
» Oxford punch needle no. 10
» Yarn – Chunky/Bulky weight, *see Chart right for suggestions, colours and amounts*
» Scissors
» Staple gun
» Staple remover or screwdriver and pliers
» Pencil
» Design template - sheet 1A
» Fabric glue (optional)
» Ribbon
» Bell
» Pipe cleaners
» Canvas for backing, 40cm (16in) square
» Toy stuffing

YARN CHART			
COLOUR	BRAND /COMPANY	CODE	AMOUNT NEEDED
Grey	Kartopu Punto (Bulky/100g - 110m)	K920	50g (1.75oz)
Purple	Kartopu Cozy Wool (Bulky/100g - 110m)	K1707	20g (0.7oz)
Cream	Kartopu Punto (Bulky/100g - 110m)	M025	20g (0.7oz)
Black	Kartopu Punto (Bulky/100g - 110m)	K940	10g (0.3oz)
Pink	Kartopu Punto (Bulky/100g - 110m)	M374	10g (0.3oz)

EMBROIDERY

1 Stretch your fabric on the frame with a staple gun (see page 20). Monk's cloth can fray easily at the edges, so it's a good idea to cut your fabric 1 – 2cm (⅜ – ¾in) wider all round than usual. A frame of 40 x 40cm (16 x 16in) will give you enough room to work comfortably.

2 Place your design template under the frame, taping it in position to keep it fixed. Hold the frame up to a light source and you will see the design through the fabric. Transfer the design to the fabric by tracing over it with a pencil (see page 21).

3 Thread your needle with black yarn and embroider the mouth, nose and eyes. When you first begin, do not forget to pull the end of the yarn to the back with your hand. You don't need to do this for sections where you embroider a single row, such as the eyes.

4 Thread your punch needle with the purple yarn and fill in the stripes of the cat and the tips of her feet. When filling in a shape, embroider the outline first and then continue to fill it in by following that outline.

5 Continue to embroider the details, using the pink, dark gray, purple and white yarns. The rule here is the inside-out rule – embroider the small details inside first and then fill in the background.

6 Finally, thread your needle with light grey yarn and embroider all the background by following the outline of the cat.

7 After completing the embroidery, trim any starting and finishing yarn ends so they are even with the fluffy part. Remove your project from the frame with the staple remover. Trim the edges of fabric, leaving an allowance of at least 4cm (10in) all round.

8 You can fix your embroidery by spreading glue on the back, but you should keep in mind that the glue will harden a little after it dries. As this is a toy for kids, I wanted it to stay soft and so I didn't use glue. Since we will sew lining to the back, the chance of the work unravelling is slim.

MAKING UP THE STUFFED TOY

1 For the cat's tail, hold five pipe cleaners together and wrap them tightly with purple yarn. Since pipe cleaners are made of wire, you can shape the tail easily as wished later on.

2 Use the design template to cut out a piece of fabric for the back panel, adding on 3cm (1¼in) all round for an allowance. Lay your embroidery out flat with the fluffy part on top. Place the tail on top, in the position you want it but with the tail facing inwards. Place the canvas fabric for the back panel on top, right sides together, and pin together.

3 Using a sewing machine, sew around the edges, stitching as close to the embroidered stitches as possible and leaving a gap of about 12cm (4¾in) in the bottom edge. Once you finish sewing, snip into any curved edges then turn the cat right side through the gap and fill it with toy stuffing.

4 When you have added the stuffing, use a sewing needle and thread to sew the gap closed using small stitches.

5 Tie a length of ribbon around the cat's neck and fasten in a bow. You can attach a bell to the ribbon if liked.

KIDS BACKPACK

Children's bags were among the projects I made most often when I first started punch needle embroidery. I usually designed shoulder bags, but although they were very cute, they were not very practical for kids. So I decided to make a backpack that children can use at school or kindergarten. I've also chosen a looped, bouclé yarn to show the different types of yarns that can be used in punch needle embroidery and to create a design that looks like a cuddly bear.

Finished Size: 23 x 23cm (9 x 9in)

MATERIALS & TOOLS

» Cotton burlap, 40cm (16in) square
» Wooden frame, 25 x 35cm (10 x 14in)
» DMC punch needle no. 10
» Adjustable punch needle (fine)
» Yarn – Bouclé and 4 ply/Sport weight, *see Chart right for suggestions, colours and amounts*
» Scissors
» Staple gun
» Staple remover or screwdriver and pliers
» Pencil
» Design template - sheet 1B
» Fabric glue (optional)
» Black and beige felt
» Sewing needle and thread
» Hot glue gun and silicone
» Zip, 35cm long
» Canvas fabric for the backing, 50cm (20in) square
» Cotton tape, 3cm (1¼in) wide, 1m (39in) for straps
» Two adjustable buckles
» Sewing machine
» Iron

YARN CHART			
COLOUR	BRAND / COMPANY	CODE	AMOUNT NEEDED
Fluffy Brown	Kartopu Anakuzusu	K883	50g (1.75oz)
Cream	Alize Cotton Gold (Fine/100g - 330m)	1	15g (0.5oz)
Black	Alize Cotton Gold (Fine/100g - 330m)	60	10g (0.3oz)
Beige	Alize Cotton Gold (Fine/100g - 330m)	67	20g (0.7g)

EMBROIDERY

1 Stretch your fabric on the frame with a staple gun (see page 20). As this is a kid's backpack, the design is fairly small so a frame with an interior width of 30 x 30cm (12 x 12in) will be big enough for you to work comfortably.

2 Place your design template under the frame, taping it around the edges to keep it fixed in place if necessary. The design will be visible on the front of the fabric when you hold the frame up to a light source. Transfer the design to the fabric by tracing over it with a pencil. Since cotton burlap is slightly thicker than other embroidery linens, it might not be so easy to see the design. If that happens you can also use carbon paper for transferring the design. Note that the head and ears are embroidered as separate pieces so draw them separately.

3 Thread an adjustable needle with black yarn and set it to 6. Start by working the nose. Do not forget to pull the starting yarn to the back with your hand. After completing the nose, embroider the mouth in a double row.

4 Remove the black yarn from your needle and thread it with cream. Fill in the space around the mouth and nose.

5 Once you have completed the mouth and nose, thread your needle with beige yarn and fill in the ears that you drew apart from the head. Embroider the outline of the ears first and then continue to fill in by following the outline. Continue to keep the setting of your needle at 6.

6 Thread your DMC needle with the bouclé yarn and use this to fill in all the head. Because this yarn has a fluffy, looped texture, it may not move easily through your needle. If this is a problem, I recommend that when you push the needle into the fabric you keep hold of the yarn at the back with your hand to help keep the yarn moving through the needle comfortably.

7 Once you've finished all the embroidery, trim any starting and finishing yarn ends so they are even with the loops.

8 Remove your finished project from the frame with the help of staple remover or a screwdriver and pliers. Cut out the head and ears separately, leaving an allowance of at least 3cm (1¼in) all round. Brush glue over the back and leave to dry for 24 hours.

MAKING UP THE BACKPACK

1 Lay the embroidered ears out flat, fluffy side down. Meanwhile, set your hot glue gun to warm up. Snip small notches around the curved upper edges of each ear, but not on the straight bottom edges. Fold the notched pieces in and glue in place with the hot glue gun. Do not turn under the bottom edges.

2 Use the ear template to cut out two pieces of beige felt. Using a needle and thread, stitch a piece of felt to the back of each embroidered ear, leaving the bottom edges unstitched.

3 Cut out two 37 x 6cm (14½ x 2¼in) pieces of canvas fabric. Turn under one long edge on each piece by 1cm (1¼in) and press in place. Open the zip and pin one edge to the folded edge of one fabric strips. Sew in place.

4 Pin the other edge of the zip to the folded edge of the other fabric strip and sew in place. Close the zip.

5 Cut out a 37 x 11cm (14½ x 4¼in) piece of canvas. Turn under the short edges by 1cm (1¼in) and press in place. Place one of these folded edges along one short edge of the piece you have joined with the zip; pin, then sew in place. You now have a strip 72 x 11cm (29 x 4¼in) long. Leave the other end unstitched; you will use this to turn the bag so we will close the gap later.

6 Lay the embroidered head out flat, right side up. Place the ears on top, right side down, so they are in the right position, with the unstitched edge of the ears lined up with the edge of the fabric; pin in place. Pin the long piece of fabric with the zip around the edge of the head, right sides together and with the zip running around the top of the head. Using a sewing machine, sew in place, stitching as close to the embroidered stitches as possible and stitching through the ears.

7 Using the head template, cut out a piece of canvas, adding at least 1cm (1¼in) of seam allowance all round, for the back panel. Lay the back panel out flat, right side up. Cut a 12cm (4¾in) length of cotton tape and shape it into a loop for the handle. Pin the ends of the tape to the edge of the back panel, at the top, positioned a short distance apart and with the loop facing in towards the centre of the fabric. Cut two 40cm (16cm) lengths of tape for straps. Pin one end of one strap to the top edge of the back panel, close to the handle, then pin the other end to a point on the opposite edge of the back panel. Repeat to pin the other strap piece in place. The handle and straps will be on top of the right side of the back panel.

8 Pin the back panel to the other side of the zipped piece, right sides together – the handle and straps will be inside.

9 Using a sewing machine, sew all round the edge of the back panel, stitching through the ends of the straps. Oversew the seams for a neat finish.

10 One end of the fabric strip with the zip was left unstitched; use this gap to access the zip and open it. Hand stitch the gap closed and then turn the bag right side out through the zip. Press the seams out with your fingers.

11 Cut out two eyes from black felt and stick them on the face of the bear with the hot glue gun.

12 Cut the straps in half and then rejoin with adjustable buckles.

RAINBOW CUSHION

There is no limit to the cushions you can make with the punch needle, all you need is a little imagination. Cushions have always been among my favourite projects to make, especially round ones, embroidered with the punch needle and combined with pompoms for a wonderful finished result. For this project, I created a round pillow decorated with a different interpretation of the rainbow motif.

Finished Size: 37cm (14½in) diameter

MATERIALS & TOOLS

» Embroidery linen, 60cm (24in) square
» Wooden frame, 50cm (20in) square
» Adjustable punch needle
» Yarn – DK/Light Worsted and 4 ply/Sport weight, *see Chart right for suggestions, colours and amounts*
» Scissors
» Staple gun
» Staple remover or screwdriver and pliers
» Pencil
» Design template - sheet 1B
» Fabric glue (optional)
» Zip, 40cm (16in)
» Canvas fabric for the backing 50cm (20in)
» About 17 small pompoms
» Sewing needle and thread
» Sewing machine

YARN CHART			
COLOUR	BRAND / COMPANY	CODE	AMOUNT NEEDED
Orange	Kartopu no.1 (Medium/100g - 160m)	K1321	40g (1.4oz)
White	Alize Cotton Gold (Fine/100g - 330m)	55	100g (3.5oz)
Pink	Alize Cotton Gold (Fine/100g - 330m)	393	25g (0.8g)
Blue	Kartopu no.1 (Fine/100g - 330m)	K1467	40g (1.4oz)
Beige	Alize Cotton Gold (Medium/100g - 160m)	67	25g (0.8g)
Yellow	Alize Cotton Gold (Fine/100g - 330m)	2	15g (0.5oz)

EMBROIDERY

1 Stretch your fabric on the frame with a staple gun. The diameter of this cushion is 45cm (18in); it is not always easy to find a round embroidery hoop this size so that's why I've used a 50 x 50cm (20 x 20in) wooden frame for this project.

2 Transfer the design to the fabric either by using carbon paper or by placing it under the frame and tracing over the design (see page 21).

3 Adjust your needle to 6 and keep it at this setting during the entire embroidery. If you want a slightly fluffier finish, you can increase the setting to 7 or 8. However, the higher your setting, the more yarn will use, so keep this in mind.

4 Thread your needle with white yarn and begin by working the inner sections of the rainbow motifs. Do not forget to pull the yarn to the back when starting. Remember that the starting and finishing ends of yarn should stay in the fluffy section, except for when you embroider a single line.

5 Beginning with beige, continue to embroider the rainbows, working outwards. When filling in an area that has small shapes inside it – like the blue stripe – fill in the small shapes first. If you filled in the blue first, the fluffy loops could cover the areas you want to fill with beige and you would have difficulty embroidering these spots.

6 When you have finished embroidering both rainbows, thread the needle with white yarn again and fill in the area between. While embroidering this area, you can work in rows or you can follow the shape of the rainbows.

7 Remove your finished project from the frame using a staple remover or a screwdriver and pliers. Trim the edges of fabric, leaving an allowance of at least 3cm (1¼in) all round.

8 Because all the areas of this cushion are filled with stitching, the loops are very tight and hold each other in place. It's unlikely, therefore, that you will need to use glue. However, if you wish, you can brush fabric glue on the back and leave to dry for 24 hours.

MAKING UP THE CUSHION

1 Use the design template to cut out a piece of fabric, 3cm (1¼in) wider all round, for the backing.

2 You can stitch the zip around the edge of the cushion if liked, but I prefer to insert it in the centre of the back panel. Cut the backing panel in half. Turn under the straight edges of each piece by 1cm (⅜in) and press in place. Open the zip and pin one edge to the folded edge of one fabric semi-circle; sew in place. Sew the other edge of the zip to the folded edge of the other fabric piece.

3 Partially close the zip, leaving about 10cm (4in) open. Bring the backing and the finished embroidery right sides together and pin all round. Sew, stitching as close to the stitched loops as possible.

4 Next, trim off any excess fabric and snip into the seam allowance all round. If liked, you can stabilise the seam by adding zigzag stitching all round or by brushing on some fabric glue. Open the zip completely and turn the cushion cover to the right side through the gap.

5 After turning your cushion to the right side, hand stitch pompoms around the edges at approximately 5cm (2in) intervals. While doing this, you can also apply some fabric glue to the pompoms to make them more durable.

HANGING WALL BANNER

Children's rooms are not just a place in which to play, they're also the space where children get a chance to shape their personality for the first time. With that in mind, when I'm creating a decorative project for a kid's room, I try to make something that will contribute to their creativity and add colour to their world – just like this banner! I aimed to make a wall hanging suitable for the room that's at the centre of many children's imaginations.

Finished Size: 40 x 55cm (16 x 21½in)

MATERIALS & TOOLS

» Duck linen fabric, 60cm (24in) square
» Wooden frame, 50cm (20in) square
» Adjustable punch needle
» Yarn – DK/Light Worsted and 4 ply/Sport weight, *see Chart right for suggestions, colours and amounts*
» Scissors
» Staple gun
» Staple remover or screwdriver and pliers
» Pencil
» Design template - sheet 2A
» Glue (optional)
» Two strips of wood, each 3cm (1¼in) wide and 45cm (18in) long
» Cotton cord, for hanging
» Sewing machine

YARN CHART			
COLOUR	BRAND / COMPANY	CODE	AMOUNT NEEDED
Nayv Blue	Yarnart Jeans (Fine/50g - 160m)	47	15g (0.5oz)
Lilac	Yarnart Jeans (Fine/50g - 160m)	19	15g (0.5oz)
Orange	Yarnart Jeans (Fine/50g - 160m)	96	20g (0.7g)
Light Orange	Yarnart Jeans (Fine/50g - 160m)	88	10g (0.3oz)
Pink	Alize Cotton Gold (Fine/100g - 330m)	393	10g (0.3oz)
Turquoise	Alize Cotton Gold (Fine/100g - 330m)	610	10g (0.3oz)
Beige	Alize Cotton Gold (Fine/100g - 330m)	67	10g (0.3oz)
Khaki	Alize Cotton Gold (Fine/100g - 330m)	485	10g (0.3oz)
Yellow	Alize Cotton Gold (Fine/100g - 330m)	2	15g (0.5oz)
Cream	Alize Cotton Gold (Fine/100g - 330m)	1	10g (0.3oz)

EMBROIDERY

1 Since we will not fill the background in this project, I've chosen to use duck linen which has a less open weave. Stretch the fabric on the frame with the help of a staple gun. The more taut your fabric, the easier it will be for you to embroider.

2 Transfer your design template to your fabric by placing it under the frame and tracing over the design, or with the help of carbon paper. In this project, we will be using both the fluffy and the flat side, so we will be embroidering on both sides of the frame. Therefore, the words 'Dreams' and 'here' should be drawn on the front and the word 'grow' on the back. Since we will use the flat side for 'grow', we can draw the text as it is. However, since we will use the fluffy side for the words 'dreams' and 'here', horizontally flipped versions of the lettering are provided (see page 21 for reversing text).

3 After transferring the design to the fabric, adjust your needle to 6. Since all the letters are separate, you can start with which one you wish. Remember to fill the inner parts first. I suggest that you fill in common colours first to save time. For example, you can thread your needle with navy blue and embroider the word 'grow', then turn the frame over and continue by filling in the middle of the letters 'M' and the lower case 'e' without changing the yarn.

4 Although the centres of 'M' and 'E' look like they are single lines, I recommend that you embroider them in a double row, so they are clearer.

5 After you've filled in all the letters, trim the starting and finishing ends yarns so they are even with the loops.

6 Remove the banner from the frame with the help of the staple remover or a screwdriver and pliers.

MAKING UP THE BANNER

1 After removing your project from the frame, lay it out flat so the fluffy part is uppermost. Turn under the right and left edges by 1cm (⅜in) inside and press. Using a sewing machine, stitch along the pressed edges to create a neat finish.

2 After sewing the edges, turn under the top and bottom edges by 3cm (1¼in); press. Place one of the wooden strips on a flat surface and lay the banner on top, wrong side up, so the top turned edge is lying on the wooden strip. Use a staple gun to secure the fabric to the wooden strip. Repeat at the bottom edge.

3 Staple a length of cotton cord to the upper wooden strip, on the back. Cotton cord is idea for this because it won't stretch too much. Use the cord to hang your banner.

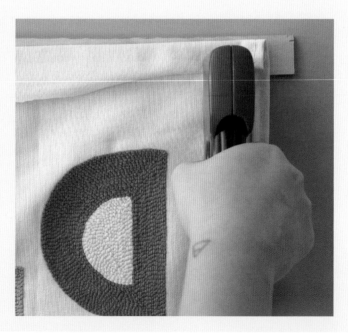

BABY BLANKET

Because the fabric that's embroidered with a punch needle needs be taut, it's better, generally speaking, to use one that does not stretch. There are ways, however, that can allow you to use different kinds of fabric with punch needle projects. By making appliqué patches in various sizes, you can apply them to any kind of cloth you want. In order to demonstrate this approach, I've created a baby blanket, decorated with cute animal motifs. This is one of the most adaptable projects in this book because you could also turn these animal shapes into other makes, such as brooches, hair clips or key rings.

Finished Size: 100 x 100cm (39 x 39in)

MATERIALS & TOOLS

» Embroidery linen, 60cm (24in) square
» Wooden frame, 50cm (20in) square
» Adjustable punch needle
» Yarn – DK/Light Worsted and 4 ply/Sport weight, *see Chart right for suggestions, colours and amounts*
» Scissors
» Staple gun
» Staple remover or screwdriver and pliers
» Pencil
» Design template - see pages 126–127
» Fabric glue (optional)
» Hot glue gun and silicone
» Piece of white or cream fleece fabric, 100cm (39in) square
» Yarn for finishing the blanket edge
» Sewing needle and thread
» Four white or cream pompoms

YARN CHART			
COLOUR	Brand/Company	CODE	Amount needed
Yellow	La Mia Cottony (DK Light/50g - 120m)	P15-L015	25g (0.8g)
Red	La Mia Cottony (DK Light/50g - 120m)	P11-L011	25g (0.8g)
Black	Alize Cotton Gold (Fine/100g - 330m)	60	25g (0.8g)
Orange	Nako Pırlanta (DK Light/100g - 225m)	6733	25g (0.8g)
Brown	Hello Cotton (Fine/25g - 62,5m)	126	25g (0.8g)
White	Alize Cotton Gold (Fine/100g - 330m)	55	25g (0.8g)
Pink	Alize Cotton Gold (Fine/100g - 330m)	393	25g (0.8g)
Dusty Pink	Himalaya Super Lux (DK Light/100g - 250m)	73442	25g (0.8g)
Grey	La Mia Cottony (DK Light/50g - 120m)	P20-L020	25g (0.8g)
Blue	Hello Cotton (Fine/25g - 62,5m)	136	25g (0.8g)
Beige	Alize Cotton Gold (Fine/100g - 330m)	67	25g (0.8g)
Green	Hello Cotton (Fine/25g - 62,5m)	137	25g (0.8g)
Yellow	Alize Cotton Gold (Fine/100g - 330m)	2	25g (0.8g)
Cream	Alize Cotton Gold (Fine/100g - 330m)	1	25g (0.8g)

EMBROIDERY

1 Stretch your fabric onto the frame with a staple gun. Each animal shape is about 6 x 6cm (2½ x 2½in) in size. If you wish, you can use a 50 x 50cm (20 x 20in) frame and embroider all the shapes together. Alternatively, if you want to embroider each animal individually, a 15cm (6in) diameter embroidery hoop will be big enough.

2 Adjust your punch needle to 5 and thread it with the black yarn. Embroider details such as mouths, eyes and noses first. Since these shapes are quite small, it will be enough to punch your needle one or two times for the eyes. When you begin, do not forget to pull the yarn through to the back with your hand, although you do not need to do this in the sections that you embroider in a single row, such as the eyes.

3 Next, embroider the small areas inside the shapes before going on to fill in the rest of each one.

4 After completing the embroidery, trim the starting and finishing ends yarns so they are even with the loops. Remove the fabric from the frame using a staple remover or screwdriver and pliers. Cut out each animal shape, leaving a 2–3cm (¾–1¼in) allowance around the edges. You don't need to apply glue to the backs of the shapes because you will use fabric glue to apply the patches to the blanket.

MAKING UP THE BLANKET

1 Lay the animal shapes our flat with the fluffy parts facing downwards. Snip small notches into the curved edges of each one. In the meantime, you can set your hot glue gun to warm up.

2 Use the glue gun to apply adhesive to the tabs made by notching the edges, then fold them to the flat side of your embroidery and press them down. Try to do this neatly so that the base fabric cannot be seen at the edges. You can also use fabric glue for this purpose; I used the hot glue gun because the adhesive dries faster.

3 Once you finish gluing the edges, lay your animal shapes out on a 100cm (39in) square of fleece fabric. Before attaching the patches, experiment with different arrangements on the fabric to see which one you like the best. I had two rows of four animal shapes and two rows of three shapes, using 14 patches in total.

4 Apply fabric glue to the backs of the patches and stick them in their chosen position. When the glue is dry, if liked, use a needle and thread and small stitches to sew them in place.

5 Now use blanket stitch to finish the edge of the fleece fabric. Thread a needle with yarn knot the tail end. With the right side facing you, bring the needle to the front. Take it to the back and insert it in the back again, through the same hole, then draw it through so you have a loop over the fabric edge. Insert the needle in the top of this loop, along the edge of the fabric, from right to left. Then insert the needle a little to the left, about 1cm below the edge and from front to back; loop the thread over the needle and pull the yarn through to tighten the stitch along the edge of the fabric. Continue in this way to work blanket stitch around the fabric edge (see below).

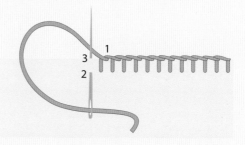

6 To complete your blanket, sew pompoms to the corners.

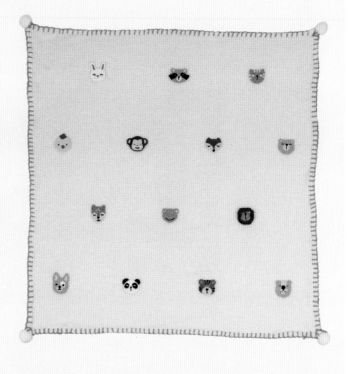

TABLE RUNNER

Everyone enjoys spending time eating with their loved ones, seated around a beautifully presented table. So when designing this project, I tried to come up with a stylish runner that would enhance any dining table. I wanted to achieve a simple elegance by embroidering some minimal, Scandinavian-style flowers on a length of raw linen. This runner is probably one of the easiest projects you will find in this book, but the fact that even a simple flower motif can turn a plain fabric into a thing of beauty demonstrates the versatility of punch needle embroidery.

Finished Size: 52 x 120cm (20½ x 48in)

MATERIALS & TOOLS

» Raw linen fabric, 55 x 120cm (21½ x 48in)
» Round embroidery hoop, 25cm (10in)
» Adjustable punch needle
» Yarn – DK/Light Worsted and 4 ply/Sport weight, *see Chart right for suggestions, colours and amounts*
» Scissors
» Pencil
» Design template - see page 122
» Fabric glue
» Sewing machine

YARN CHART			
COLOUR	Brand / Company	CODE	Amount needed
Black	Alize Cotton Gold (Fine/100g - 330m)	60	50g (1.75oz)
Orange	Nako Pırlanta (DK Light/100g - 225m)	6733	30g (1oz)
Cream	Alize Cotton Gold (Fine/100g - 330m)	1	25g (0.8oz)

EMBROIDERY

1 As a large piece of fabric is used for this project, I recommend using a round embroidery hoop. Generally speaking, I prefer stretching fabric over a wooden frame because the all-essential tension is better. However, you can also use a round embroidery hoop; one with a diameter of 25cm (10in) will give you enough space to work comfortably on this embroidery.

2 Firstly, transfer your design to the fabric. For this project, I chose a raw linen and I transferred the design using carbon paper since it could be a little difficult to see the image on the front of the linen after placing it under the fabric. After positioning the carbon paper between the template and the fabric, go over the image with a pencil to transfer the image to the fabric.

3 Once you've transferred the design, stretch your fabric in the hoop. Place the inner part of the hoop under your fabric, centred on one flower. Then place the outer hoop on top and tighten the screw with a pair of pliers.

4 Adjust your punch needle to 6 and thread it with black yarn.

5 Embroider the stem and leaves of the flower with black yarn. When you begin, pull the yarn through to the back with your hand. Embroider the outline of the leaves first and then fill them in. Since the stem of the flower is worked in a single row, you can make stitches smaller than usual.

6 After you have finished embroidering the leaves, thread your punch needle with the cream and orange yarns respectively and complete the flower.

7 When you've finished the first flower, remove the fabric from the hoop, then reposition it, centred over the next flower. Fill in the next two flowers in the same way as the first. Work three more flowers at the other end of the runner.

8 Trim the starting and finishing ends yarns so they are even with the loops. Brush some glue over the flat side of each flower. I recommend using glue in this project because, as it is designed as a table runner, it may need to be washed frequently.

MAKING UP THE RUNNER

1 After completing your embroidery, turn under the long edges of the runner by 1cm (⅜in) and press. Using a sewing machine, stitch along the pressed edges.

2 You could hem all four edges but I decided to fringe the edges below the embroidery because the threads of linen fabrics are easily pulled out. For this fringe, I pulled out about 15 rows of horizontal threads. You could apply a thin strip of glue to the back of the runner to avoid the fringes fraying too much.

CURTAIN TIE BACK

Sometimes it's the small details that make the biggest difference. And I think that this is certainly the case with decoration. Even the smallest home decor accessories can completely transform a room's atmosphere in an instant. The curtain tie back I made for this project is an accessory created just for this purpose. I love using animal motifs, especially in children's rooms, so I designed a curtain tie back featuring a sloth and a leaf that would suit either a girl's or boy's room. However, as with every project in this book, I do not want you to limit yourself to this use – you could hang this make anywhere you wish!

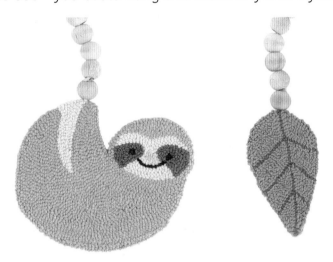

Finizhed Size: 71cm (28in) long

MATERIALS & TOOLS

» Embroidery linen, 35cm (14in) square
» Wooden frame, 30cm (12in) square
» Adjustable punch needle
» Yarn – DK/Light Worsted and 4 ply/Sport weight, *see Chart right for suggestions, colours and amounts*
» Scissors
» Staple gun
» Staple remover or screwdriver and pliers
» Pencil
» Design template - page 126
» Fabric glue (optional)
» Hot glue gun and silicone
» 8–10mm (¼–⅜in) wooden beads x 30
» Cotton cord, 60cm (24in)
» Felt for backing

YARN CHART			
Colour	Brand / Company	Code	Amount needed
Black	Alize Cotton Gold (Fine/100g - 330m)	60	5g (0.18oz)
Brown	HELLO Cotton (Fine/25g - 62,5m)	126	5g (0.18oz)
Pink	Alize Cotton Gold (Fine/100g - 330m)	393	5g (0.18oz)
Beige	Alize Cotton Gold (Fine/100g - 330m)	67	15g (0.5oz)
Green	HELLO Cotton (Fine/25g - 62,5m)	137	10g (0.3oz)
Dark Green	La Mia Cottony (DK Light/50g - 120m)	P30	5g (0.18oz)
Cream	Alize Cotton Gold (Fine/100g - 330m)	1	10g (0.3oz)

EMBROIDERY

1 Stretch your fabric on the frame with the staple gun. It is very important that your fabric is stretched tightly if you are to work on it comfortably so pull the fabric from the edges gently and staple it in place (see page 20).

2 This tie back is made up of two separate pieces; a frame of 30 x 30cm (12 x 12in) will be big enough for both. Place the design templates under the frame, hold it up to a light source and trace over the image with a pencil. Do not forget to leave at least 4cm (1½in) between the shapes so you can easily cut them out separately.

3 Adjust your needle to 5 and thread it with dark green yarn. Begin by embroidering the lines inside the leaf in single rows. You do not want the base fabric to visible between the stitches so you can make smaller stitches than usual. Also, you do not need to pull the starting thread to the back when working a single line. After completing the lines, thread your needle with light green and fill in the remainder of the leaf. Try to follow the outline of the figure while doing this, and pull the starting thread to the back with your hand when you begin.

4 When you have finished embroidering the leaf, thread your needle with black yarn and embroider sloth's mouth and eyes. Since the eye is very small, it will be sufficient to punch your needle just a few times. Then fill in the inner shapes, working with pink, cream and brown yarn, before using beige to fill in the rest of the sloth.

5 After you finished the embroidery, trim the starting and finishing ends yarns so they are even with the loops.

6 If liked, you can apply fabric glue to the wrong side of the embroidery, then wait for 24 hours for it to dry. However, this is not essential for this project, as we will cover the back of each piece with felt.

7 Remove the fabric from the frame with the help of a staple remover or a screwdriver and pliers. Cut the two pieces out, leaving at least 2cm (¾in) of allowance all round each one.

MAKING UP THE TIE BACK

1 Lay your embroidered pieces out flat with the fluffy part facing downwards. Snip small notches into the curved edges of both piece. In the meantime, you can set your hot glue gun to warm up.

2 Use the glue gun to apply adhesive to the tabs made by notching the edges, then fold them to the flat side of your work and press down. The base fabric should not be on the fluffy side. You can also use fabric glue for this although I prefer the hot glue gun because the adhesive dries faster.

3 Use your design templates to cut out the same shapes from felt. Using a sewing needle and thread, sew the felt backing pieces to the embroidered pieces, leaving a small gap at the top of each one. Fold an 8cm (3¼in) long piece of the cream yarn in half and insert it in one of the gaps for a hanging loop, then stitch in place. Repeat to add a hanging loop to the second piece.

4 Tie the sloth to one end of a 60cm (24in) long cotton cord. String 30 wooden beads onto the cord, then tie the leaf to the other end. Wrap the beaded section around around your curtain and then loop it over itself to secure.

MIRROR

One of my favourite things about punch needle embroidery is how we can use the piece we are embroidering for many different purposes. In this book, I've tried to show you the versatility of punch needle embroidery by including as many different projects as possible. Mirror making is quite common in other crafts, especially in fields such as macramé and basket weaving, so I thought it was a good idea to make a mirror featuring punch needle embroidery and I came up with this project. I've used a metallic gold yarn here to try and give more elegant finished look. Hopefully, this mirror will end up being one of the most popular pieces for your home!

Finished Size: 45cm (18in) diameter

MATERIALS & TOOLS

» Embroidery linen, 60cm (24in) square
» Wooden frame, 50cm (20in) square
» Adjustable punch needle
» Yarn – DK/Light Worsted and 4 ply/Sport weight, *see Chart right for suggestions, colours and amounts*
» Scissors
» Staple gun
» Staple remover or screwdriver and pliers
» Pencil
» Design template - sheet 1B
» Fabric glue (optional)
» Hot glue gun and silicone
» Two metal rings, one 18cm (7in) in diameter, one 45cm (18in) in diameter
» Round mirror, 19–20cm (7½–8in) diameter
» Felt, cardboard or thin wood for backing
» Cord for hanging

YARN CHART			
Colour	Brand / Company	Code	Amount needed
White	La Mia Cottony (DK Light/50g - 120m)	P3-L003	150g (5.3oz)
Gold	Diva Lurex (Super Fine/ 8m)	1	25g (0.8g)

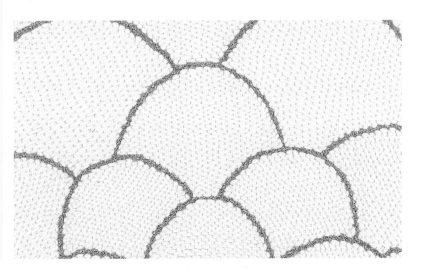

EMBROIDERY

1 Stretch your fabric on the frame with the help of a staple gun. It is very important that your fabric is taut so that you can punch your needle easily into the fabric (see page 20).

2 The finished piece is 45cm (18in) in diameter, so I recommend working with a frame at least a 50 x 50cm (20 x 20in). If you cut your fabric 5cm (2in) wider all round you will be able to staple it comfortably.

3 Transfer the design to the fabric using the template provided. The design for this mirror frame is worked between two circles; the inner circle should have a diameter of 18cm (7in), the outer one should be 45cm (18in).

4 Adjust your punch needle to 5 and thread it with the metallic gold yarn. The flat side of the work is the right side for this mirror, so I set the punch needle to 5 to keep the amount of yarn needed to a minimum.

5 When you begin, remember to pull the starting thread to the back with your hand. Embroider the gold outlines on the entire design, working two rows along each line. This will make the gold-coloured lines look a little more distinct. Don't forget to pull the finishing end of each thread to the back too.

6 After filling in the gold-coloured outlines, thread your punch needle with white yarn and keep your setting at 5. Fill in all the petal shapes one by one, using the brick method (see page 28). If you were going to use the fluffy part as the right side, I would recommend you follow the outline of a shape when filling it in, but this rule does not apply with the brick method. In order work this technique neatly, fill in the shape by punching the needle from right to left or vice versa.

7 Once you've filled in all of the design, turn the frame over and trim the starting and finishing yarns to the same length as the loops.

8 When your embroidery is finished, you can apply glue to the side you will not see and leave it to dry for 24 hours.

9 Remove your project from the frame using a staple remover or a screwdriver and pliers. Trim the fabric, making sure that there is a margin of at least 4cm (1½in) left all round.

MAKING UP THE MIRROR

1 Lay the finished piece out flat with the fluffy part on top. Cut a disc out of the centre, leaving a 4cm (1½in) margin within the inner circle. Snip notches into the outer and inner edges. In the meantime, set your hot glue gun to warm up.

2 Take the 18cm (7in) metal ring and place it in the centre of your project. Use the hot glue gun to apply adhesive to the fabric tabs around the centre, then fold these over the ring. If liked, you can sew the edges down too.

3 Place the larger metal ring on the outer edge of your finished embroidery. Apply glue to the tabs around the outer edge, then fold these over the ring. Do not pull too much on one side when gluing, because this might stretch the piece and you might not have a symmetric finish. Keep the piece taut and glue the turned-under edges so that no fabric is visible from the right side.

4 After gluing the metal rings, place a 19–20cm (7½–8in) diameter mirror in the centre of your project and glue it in place with the hot glue gun or another strong adhesive.

5 Finally, you can cover the back of the mirror with felt, cardboard or wood to make it look neat. Cut out a 45cm (18in) diameter disc from your chosen material and glue it in place; you can insert a length of cord between the backing and the mirror frame while doing this to create a hanging loop.

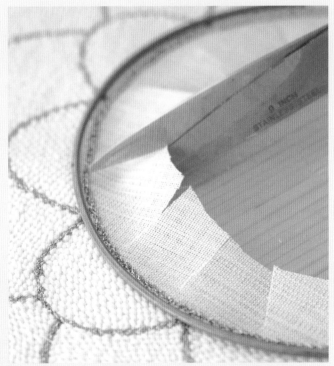

COASTERS

I do like a good cup of coffee when I'm busy crafting. I can safely say that I am something of a coffee addict and fellow addicts can appreciate how beautiful accessories, like as cups and coasters, can make this habit even more enjoyable. Moreover, I love the fact that coasters are not only decorative but practical too, protecting surfaces from damage by the hot cup. For this project, I designed three different coasters to enhance any coffee break.

Finished Size: 11cm (4¼in) diameter

MATERIALS & TOOLS

» Embroidery linen, 40cm (16in) square
» Wooden frame, 30cm (12in) square
» Adjustable punch needle
» Yarn – DK/Light Worsted and 4 ply/Sport weight, *see Chart right for suggestions, colours and amounts*
» Scissors
» Staple gun
» Staple remover or screwdriver and pliers
» Pencil
» Design template - sheet 1B
» Sewing needle
» Glue (optional)
» Clothes pegs or bulldog clips

YARN CHART			
Colour	Brand / Company	Code	Amount needed
Cream	Alize Cotton Gold (Fine/100g - 330m)	1	25g (0.8oz)
Tile Red	Gazzal Baby Cotton (Fine/50g - 165m)	3454	25g (0.8oz)
Blue	Gazzal Baby Cotton (Fine/50g - 165m)	3429	25g (0.8oz)
Dark Grey	La Mia Cottony (DK Light/50g - 120m)	P19	10g (0.3oz)

EMBROIDERY

1 Using a staple gun, stretch your fabric onto the frame. You can easily fit these three coasters in a 30 x 30cm (12 x 12in) frame.

2 Transfer your design to the fabric with a pencil or carbon paper (see page 20). You will embroider all the coasters on the same frame, so leave at least 6cm (2¼in) space between each one.

3 Adjust your punch needle to 6 and thread it with dark grey yarn. You can use a higher setting, but the loops will be more fluffy and your surface will be slightly more uneven, which might be a problem when you place a cup on a coaster.

4 Use the dark grey to embroider the leaf on the first coaster and the dots on the second one. As the leaf is worked in a single line you can make the stitches a little smaller than usual. To fill in the dots, first outline them then continue to fill with concentric circles. After filling in each dot, cut the yarn before moving on to fill the next one. In punch needle embroidery, we do not jump from shape to shape without cutting the yarn because this increases the chance of your embroidery unravelling.

5 With the setting of your punch needle still at 6, thread it with tile red yarn. Embroider the lines on the checked coaster, working in double rows. Before changing to a different colour, you can also embroider the area that needs to be filled with tile red yarn on the other coasters.

6 Thread your needle with cream yarn and embroider the shapes that need to be filled with that colour on each coaster. Follow the outline of the shapes while filling them in.

7 Finally, thread your needle with blue yarn and fill in the blue areas on the coasters.

8 Once you've completed the embroidery, remove the fabric from the frame with the staple remover or screwdriver and pliers. Cut out each coaster, leaving an allowance of at least 3cm (1¼in) all round. Trim the starting and finishing yarns to the same length as the loops, then brush the backs with fabric glue. Leave it to dry for 24 hours.

MAKING UP THE COASTERS

1 Lay the coasters out flat, with the fluffy parts facing downwards. Roll the fabric allowance of each coaster inwards, and secure with clothes pegs or bulldog clips.

2 Thread a needle with tile red yarn and tie a knot at the end. Working on the coaster with the leaf decoration, insert your needle through the back of the roll you have made on the edge of the coaster, and pull the yarn through so the knot stays on the back. Continue sewing in the same way, from back to front and all around the edge, until you have covered the rolled allowance with yarn.

3 Repeat the previous step with blue yarn for the dotty coaster and cream for the checked one.

POUFFE WITH POMPOMS

If we want a warm and cosy atmosphere at home, pouffes and cushions are among the first items that come to my mind when choosing our decor. Therefore, I wanted to create a pouffe that can be used in any part of the house. You might use this pouffe as a seat for a child, as cushion on a sofa or to rest your feet on in the living room.

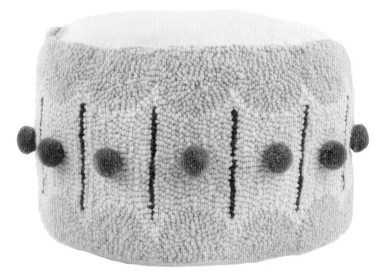

Finished Size: 40cm (16in) in diameter, 23cm (9in) tall

MATERIALS & TOOLS

» Cotton burlap, 140 x 65cm (56 x 25½in)
» Wooden frame, 65 x 30cm (25½ x 12in)
» Oxford punch needle no. 10
» Yarn – Chunky/Bulky weight, *see Chart right for suggestions, colours and amounts*
» Scissors
» Staple gun
» Staple remover or screwdriver and pliers
» Pencil
» Design template - sheet 2A
» Fabric glue
» 14 small dark orange pompoms
» Sewing machine
» Zip, 40cm (16in)
» Canvas fabric 1m (39in)
» Sewing needle and thread
» Pins
» Foam cylinder, 40cm (16in) wide and 23cm (9in) tall

YARN CHART			
Colour	Brand /Company	Code	Amount needed
Cream	Kartopu Punto (Bulky/100g - 110m)	K025	200g (7oz)
Light Green	Kartopu Cozy Wool (Bulky/100g - 110m)	K920	150g (5.3oz)
Dark Green	Kartopu Cozy Wool (Bulky/100g - 110m)	K1480	50g (1.75oz)

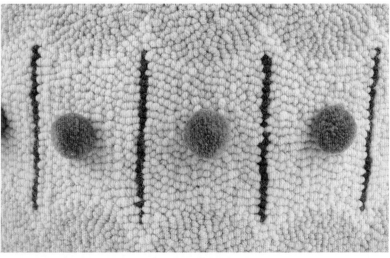

EMBROIDERY

1 This pouffe is one of the bigger projects in this book, so you need a piece of fabric 125cm (50in) long and 30cm (12in) wide. As it would be difficult to work on a frame to fit this size, I decided to make this from two separate pieces, each 75 x 35cm (30 x 14in), mounted on a 65 x 30cm (25½ x 12in) frame and then join the two pieces later.

2 Stretch the first piece of fabric on the frame with a staple gun. Make sure that the fabric is stretched tightly; the more taut your fabric is, the easier it will be to embroider.

3 Transfer the design template to your fabric by placing it under the frame, holding this up the light and then tracing over the image, or by using carbon paper. As this is not a complex design, you could also draw it freehand.

4 After transferring the design to the fabric, thread your punch needle with light green yarn. I've chosen to use an Oxford no. 10 needle in this project. You can start by filling in the scalloped areas at the top and bottom. Remember to pull the starting thread to the back with your hand.

5 Thread your punch needle with dark green yarn and embroider the single lines. Do not pull the starting and finishing ends of yarn to the back while filling these lines, these should remain on the flat side. Normally, you draw the starting and finishing ends of yarn to the fluffy side of the work, but this doesn't apply when embroidering a single line as you will get a neater finish.

6 Finally, thread your needle with cream yarn and fill in the background.

7 When the first piece is finished, remove it from the frame and set aside. Stretch the second piece of fabric on the frame and embroider as above.

8 Trim the starting and finishing yarns to the same length as the loops on both pieces. Trim the edges of both pieces leaving an allowance of at least 3cm (1¼in) all round.

9 I prefer to use fabric glue for this project, since it hardens after drying and so helps the pouffe retain its shape. After brushing the glue on the flat side, leave it to dry for 24 hours.

MAKING UP THE POUFFE

1 Lay the two pieces of embroidered fabric out flat, one on top of the other and with the fluffy parts facing. Using a needle and matching thread, hand-stitch these two pieces together. As I don't want the fabric between these two pieces to be seen, I prefer to hand sew since I can get a closer join. After combining the two pieces, you will have a large piece 30 x 125cm (12 x 50in).

2 Cut out two 40cm (16in) diameter circles from the remaining fabric you have for the top and bottom panels.

3 Pin the long embroidered piece around the edge of the top panel, right sides together.

4 Using a sewing machine, sew the pieces together, stitching as close to the embroidered stitches as possible.

5 Cut the bottom panel in half. Turn under the straight edges on each piece by 1cm (⅜in) and press.

6 Open the zip and pin one edge to the folded edge of one fabric semi-circle; sew in place. Sew the other edge of the zip to the folded edge of the other fabric semi-circle.

7 Pin the remaining edge of the long embroidered piece around the edge of the back panel, right sides together. Use the sewing machine to sew the two pieces together.

8 Open the zip by about 10cm (4in). Using a needle and thread, join the remaining short ends of the long embroidered piece. Open up the zip fully and turn the pouffe to the right side through it. Insert a cylindrical shaped foam pad.

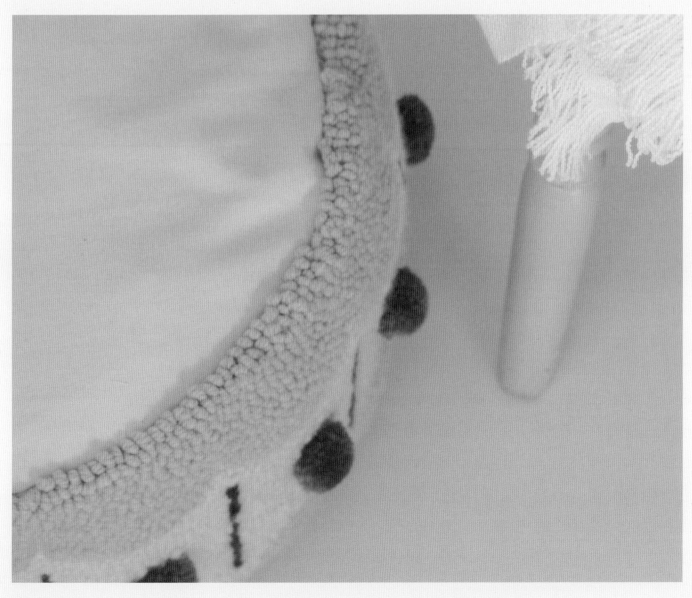

FREQUENTLY ASKED QUESTIONS

1. WHY ARE MY STITCHES COMING OUT?

If the yarn comes back out of the fabric with the punch needle when you push in the needle, there may be two main reasons for this problem. Firstly, you may not have the right needle-to-fabric match. We do not fasten anything with knots in punch needle embroidery; all we do is to push the needle in and pull it out. Therefore, the compatibility of your chosen the fabric to your needle is very important. The weave of your fabric should be open enough for the needle to pass through easily, but tight enough to hold onto the yarn. If the yarn comes out when you pull the punch needle out, the holes between the weave of your fabric may be bigger than your needle. For example, if you try to embroider with a fine needle on a fabric with large holes, such as burlap, the yarn is likely to come out with the needle as it is pulled.

Another reason could be your yarn is getting stuck. The yarn you use during punch needle embroidery should be able to move freely through the needle. For this reason, make sure that your yarn is not caught on anything while you work.

2. HOW CAN I CLEAN A PROJECT THAT I'VE MADE WITH THE PUNCH NEEDLE?

You can clean a project you have embroidered with a punch needle by washing in your machine on the hand-wash setting, or washing it by hand, depending on the care instructions of your chosen yarn. You can clean the wall hanging or garland style projects by wiping them with a damp cloth..

3. I MADE A MISTAKE WHILE EMBROIDERING, WHAT CAN I DO?

Punch needle embroidery is perhaps one of few the crafts which tolerates mistakes easily. When you do something wrong or your embroidery isn't what you want, you can gently pull your needle out of the fabric and then pull the yarn to undo the stitching until you reach the point you want to return to. Once you have undone the mistake, slowly draw the needle back down the long thread to the fabric surface and continue embroidering. Also, sometimes when inserting your punch needle in the fabric, it can raise a loop in the previous line of stitching. If this happens, I recommend you remove the bit where you went wrong if you are still close to it. However, if the loop is only slightly raised, I suggest you continue to work and the trim the raised section even with the other loops when the project is finished.

4. WHERE SHOULD I START?

We can divide the designs for punch needle embroidery into two categories. The first one consists of designs that are made of shapes within shapes figures; the second consists of designs made up of several separate shapes. In the first category, we must start by filling the innermost shapes. For example, with the cat toy (see page 80), we first need to embroider the little details such as the mouth, nose and eyes. If we started with filling in the background, the fluffy loops can obscure the area where we want to embroider the details. For the second category, it is possible to start from any point when shapes are separate. Fill in the separate shapes first, then embroider the background. For example, the book cover on page 60 features many different shapes. You can start by filling in the triangle or the circle. Once you've filled in all the shapes, you can then embroider the background.

5. IS IT ESSENTIAL TO USE GLUE?

In punch needle embroidery, we create a loop every time we punch the needle. When you embroider a single line, you may feel as if the stitches might be pulled out, but as the project progresses, the loops will start to hold together. The risk, therefore, of the stitches unravelling is very low. However, the application of glue to the reverse of your work can give added security. It should be borne in mind that, when the glue dries, it hardens a little. Generally speaking, I do not use glue in projects that I do not need to clean frequently, such as wall hangings, or in those projects where I add a lining. I prefer glue for items that I need to clean more often, such as rugs and cushions.

https://youtu.be/ZH59R5x9KZY

DESIGNS

Pot Holder
Page 40

Pot Holder
Page 40

Table Runner
Page 100

Garland
Page 64

Garland
Page 64

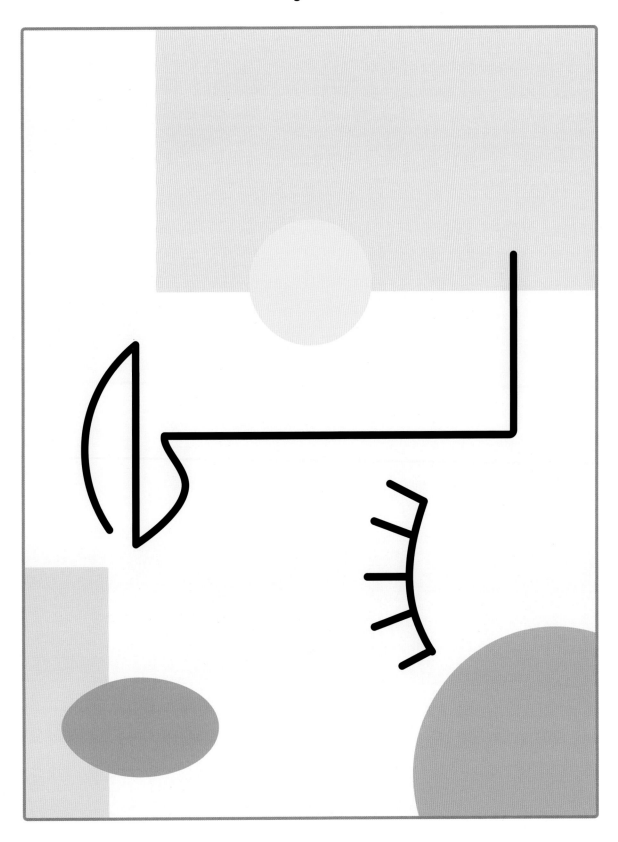

Curtain Tie Back
Page 104